Assessment in Physical Education: A Teacher's Guide to the Issues

Assessment in Physical Education:
A Teacher's Guide to the Issues

Bob Carroll

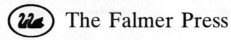

The Falmer Press

(A member of the Taylor & Francis Group)
London • Washington, D.C.

UK The Falmer Press, 4 John St, London WC1N 2ET
USA The Falmer Press, Taylor & Francis Inc., 1900 Frost Road, Suite 101, Bristol, PA 19007

First published 1994

A catalogue record for this book is available from the British Library

Library of Congress Cataloging-in-Publication Data are available on request

ISBN 0 7507 0298 2 cased
ISBN 0 7507 0299 0 paperback

Jacket design by Caroline Archer
Set in 9.5/11pt Times by
Graphicraft Typesetters Ltd, Hong Kong

Printed in Great Britain by Burgess Science Press, Basingstoke on paper which has a specified pH value on final paper manufacture of not less than 7.5 and is therefore 'acid free'.

Contents

List of Abbreviations

AEB	Associated Examining Board
AT	Attainment Target
APU	Assessment of Performance Unit
BAGA	British Amateur Gymnastics Association
BCPE	British Council of Physical Education
BTEC	Business and Technology Education Council
CCPR	Central Council for Physical Recreation
CEE	Certificate of Extended Education
C&G, CGLI	City and Guilds of London Institute
CPVE	Certificate of Pre-Vocational Education
CSE	Certificate of Secondary Education
DES	Department of Education and Science
DFE	Department For Education
EOC	Equal Opportunities Commission
ES	End of Key Stage Statement
GCE	General Certificate of Education
GCSE	General Certificate of Secondary Education
GNVQ	General National Vocational Qualifications
HMI	Her Majesty's Inspectorate
HMSO	Her Majesty's Stationery Office
ILB	Industry Lead Body
INSET	In-Service Training
ILAM	Institute of Leisure Amenity Managers
KS	Key Stages
LEA	Local Education Authority
LEAG	London and East Anglian Examining Group (now ULEAC)
MEG	Midlands Examining Group
NCC	National Curriculum Council
NCVQ	National Council for Vocational Qualifications
NEA	Northern Examining Association (now NEAB)
NEAB	Northern Examinations and Assessment Board
NISEAC	Northern Ireland Schools Examinations and Assessment Council
NPRA	Northern Partnership for Records of Achievement
NVQ	National Vocational Qualifications

PE   Physical Education
POS   Programmes of Study
ROA   Records of Achievement
SCRE   Scottish Council for Research in Education
SEAC   Schools Examinations and Assessment Council
SEG   Southern Examining Group
SCOTVEC   Scottish Council for Vocational Education
SHA   Secondary Heads Association
TVEI   Technical and Vocational Education Initiative
TGAT   Task Group on Assessment and Testing

Acknowledgments

The following have been reprinted with the kind permission of those mentioned below:

Table 8   The Secretary of the NEAB
Table 20   The Secretary of the MEG
Table 24   The Editor of the Bulletin of PE
Figure 8   The Headmaster and Head of PE at Great Sankey High School
Figure 10 The Headmaster and Head of PE at Barden High School
Figure 12 The NCC

Preface

This book is for all teachers who teach physical education in schools and colleges. It is also aimed at those who train teachers and are involved in the professional development of teachers. In the past assessment was always underplayed or even neglected in the training of PE teachers. This is not surprising as PE was not traditionally in the formal structures of assessment until recently. However, all that has changed with the advent of GCSE, ROA and the National Curriculum. Therefore no-one in PE can afford to neglect this area any more. However, teachers becoming involved in these developments usually have a lot of questions to ask and issues to clarify. Books on assessment in education have completely ignored physical education and the particular issues which are raised by the PE context. This book has been written to fill that gap, and hopefully will meet teachers' needs and those of their trainers and professional developers. It has been written in the form of posing and answering teachers' questions, such as, 'Why assess?'; 'What can I assess?'; 'How can I assess satisfactorily in PE?'; 'What type of ROA's are there?'; 'Can the National Curriculum be delivered in primary schools?'; 'What are the effects of all this assessment?' The issues raised by these questions are discussed in some detail. Therefore it is not a simple 'how to do it' book. This may disappoint some teachers because, in the demanding world of the school and with the ever increasing demands of the Government, a simple recipe for handling assessment and its issues is attractive. This may be particularly so for the hard pressed primary teacher. This book may, therefore, seem complex for many teachers. However, I suggest that in order to arrive at a simple, yet effective, recipe, teachers must consider the relevant issues. I believe they will also find it useful in two ways. Firstly, they will find practical advice, and secondly they will find that it has a relation to assessment in other subjects and issues in the school more generally.

As teachers will be aware, this has not been an easy time to write about assessment because the situation has been constantly changing. During the writing of this book, the interim report of the working party for PE and the statutory orders for PE have been published, Ministers of Education have been changed, and the Government was always making new pronouncements on some aspect of assessment to do with the National Curriculum or examinations or vocational qualifications. Two examining groups changed their names recently as well. It was like trying to catch an elusive fly. A more apt description in relation to PE might be: it was like trying to find where the goal posts had been moved to and what game those goal posts belonged to.

This book is the result of my involvement in assessment in PE over a long period of time in many capacities; firstly, as a teacher; secondly, as a teacher trainer and professional developer; thirdly, as a researcher; and fourthly, as someone involved in the development of examinations. All these roles have helped me to a greater knowledge and understanding of assessment from the theoretical and practical points of view. I have tried to pass on some of this knowledge and understanding in this book, hopefully in a form which will be useful to teachers. However, I have benefited enormously from all my contacts with teachers, students, pupils and examining board staff over the years and I am indebted to them. I am also grateful to reviewers who have kindly commented on the script, particularly to Steve Brook and Tom Christie; to Joyce Carroll for her help with the text; and Miriam Fox for help with the tables and figures: to Joyce and the rest of my family for their unswerving support during this project and the years of my professional development.

Chapter 1

What is This Thing Called 'Assessment' all About?

The Context

Indeed it would be no exaggeration to say that the 1980s have been the era of assessment-led education reform. (Hargreaves, 1989, p. 99)

Although assessment had often been the focus of educational debate and reform, for example, the 11+ examination, and the introduction of CSE, I think it is fair to say that assessment debate and reform had never been tackled on so many fronts, so continuously, so pervasively and so far reaching as those during the 1980s. During this period there had been three main initiatives and reform, the GCSE, Records Of Achievement (ROA) and the National Curriculum. There had been a long build-up to the amalgamation of the GCE and CSE to form the GCSE, and with it came more fundamental change from norm referencing to criterion referencing which has changed teachers' thinking on testing in other situations and for all ages. At approximately the same time, Government pilot schemes of ROA were taking place because of the dissatisfaction with examination results and certificates, along with the oft discredited and non-compulsory school reports, as the only means of showing what had been achieved at school. But, of course, ROA does not just target the fifth year leaving pupil in that year. In future it will target the pupils' achievement throughout the school years. After an 'on-off' situation, recording and reporting to parents finally became part of Government policy.

The most far reaching of all is, of course, the National Curriculum with its assessments at the end of four key stages (ages 7, 11, 14 and 16). There have been other initiatives too, such as CPVE and TVEI with their links to employment, modularization of courses with certification by examination groups and LEAs, and discussion on the reform of sixth form and advanced level courses. Post-16 and advanced level reform is likely to be the most controversial and heated debate of the early 1990s. However, the most contentious issues and heated debate in the pre-16 school years concern the assessments in the National Curriculum and these have occurred because of management problems and because of conflicting purposes and interests. These are issues which affect physical education no less than other subjects so will be themes which will be tackled in this book.

What all these initiatives have done is to bring assessment, which had always been at the heart of teaching, to the forefront of educational and political debate and policy. The reasons for this are complex and have been analyzed by Hargreaves (1989). He refers to the crisis of motivation. At the heart are the crises of confidence in standards and in the schools' instrumental economic function of providing a suitable work force. What it means for teachers is that they have become much more involved in formal assessment techniques and procedures and need to have greater understanding of what is involved.

In the past, assessment debate and reform hardly touched PE directly. PE teachers were often left to their own devices in curriculum and assessment matters. Annual school reports with limited space for comment, and the selection of schools teams, were usually the only formal or open assessment which had to be made. It was not until the 1970s that some PE teachers became involved in examinations through the CSE, but it was the advent of the GCSE which brought substantial numbers of schools and PE teachers into the examination scene (Carroll, 1990a). Many more are about to become involved. Many PE teachers found that they had to get involved in assessment through ROA and many more will have to do so. Primary school teachers will have to get involved in ROA as, so far, few have done so (DES, 1991d) and this includes PE recording. The National Curriculum requirements will involve both primary and secondary teachers in the assessment of pupils in PE, recording that assessment at the end of the four key stages, and to carry out more formative assessments in between in accordance with the subject group's proposals (DES, 1991a) and statutory orders (DES, 1992). There is an increasing number of PE teachers involved in more specialist assessment through GCSE, 'A' level PE and Sport Studies, and BTEC Leisure Studies, at both theoretical and practical levels (see Carroll, 1990a, and chapter 6). However, most PE teachers have had no initial training whatsoever in assessment techniques, nor had they normally been used to formally assessing their pupils, though formal testing had been used for some time in governing bodies of sport awards schemes, such as those of the Gymnastics Association (BAGA Awards). Teachers had, of course, been used to assessing as part of the normal teaching situation, but assessment itself had rarely been a focal point. In the teaching situation, assessment was just taken for granted. A massive in-service programme and 'learn on the job' was, and still is, required for teachers to understand the issues and cope with the practical problems of carrying out the assessments. Hopefully this book will play a small part in that development. It is necessary, I feel, firstly, to treat assessment as problematic and discuss what it is all about, that is, its nature, principles, modes etc., in order to give readers a better understanding of assessment, clarify its terminology and purpose before discussing physical education in more detail in later chapters. This approach will give readers a better basis for undertaking and understanding assessment.

In this book, the terms 'practical' and 'theoretical' are used in relation to pupils' assessment and work. They are terms which are in common usage in physical education and the meanings are normally taken for granted. However, there are different meanings in their usage and sometimes confusion in the use of the terms. In this book 'practical' refers to a physically active context as in the practical performance of an activity such as gymnastics or games, whilst 'theoretical' refers to knowledge, ideas, etc., about aspects of PE, such as knowledge of rules, knowledge of the effects of exercise shown in a non-practical way.

What is Assessment?

Some books which set out to define assessment, do not in fact do that, but instead end up discussing the purposes or uses of assessment. For a better understanding of assessment, a distinction must be made between what assessment is, its purposes and its uses, and in teaching and education it is necessary to clarify these in the practical situation. Even some of the best books on the subject are not always precise enough, for example, Rowntree (1977) which is still one of the best discussions on issues, and Satterly (1989), which is one of the most technically useful and more up-to-date.

Satterly (1989) describes educational assessment as 'an omnibus term which includes all the processes and products which describe the nature and extent of children's learning, its degree of correspondence with the aims and objectives of teaching and its relationship with the environments which are designed to facilitate learning' (p. 3).

This is both a global and limiting description at the same time, yet it does not say what assessment actually is. Its limiting factor is that it just relates to learning, and this is clearly seen by Satterly as the educational aspect. Yet there are many other assessments made in schools and educational establishments which may not be encompassed by the term learning, for example behavioural, attitudinal, and personal.

Rowntree (1977) tells readers what assessment is,

> more basically, assessment in education can be thought of as occurring whenever one person, in some kind of interaction, direct or indirect with another, is conscious of obtaining and interpreting information about the knowledge and understanding of abilities and attitudes of that other person. (p. 4)

However, Rowntree goes on to suggest that,

> Assessment can be descriptive (for example, 'Bob knows his number bonds up to 20') without becoming judgmental (for example, 'Bob is good at number bonds'). (p. 6)

Whilst Rowntree is quite right in his examples, I am going to suggest that assessment always involves making a judgment. The key word in Rowntree's definition is 'interpretation' and for assessment to take place, that interpretation will include a judgment or a judgment will follow. So, looking at Rowntree's two examples, both of them involve making a judgment or forming an opinion. The difference is that in the second example, the teacher has placed a value, the construct 'good', on Bob's performance at number bonds. In the first instance, the teacher is saying that he has weighed up the evidence, that is, he has seen or heard Bob using or counting his number bonds, probably on several occasions, and he is of the opinion and has judged that 'Bob knows his number bonds'. The teacher's knowing includes the judgment and is an assessment of the pupil. A purely descriptive statement without judgment would be 'Bob counted up to twenty'.

Some readers may feel that this is merely a semantic difference, but I do not think so. I want to stress the differences only so far as they are fundamental to the understanding of what assessment is all about. Statements such as the examples given by Rowntree actually say a lot more than the mere words themselves, and they include more judgments and assessments than appear at first sight. Take, for example, the following statements by a teacher in the physical education context:

    A. 'Liz passed the ball.'
    B. 'Liz can pass the ball.'
    C. 'Liz gave a very good pass'.

Statement A is purely descriptive, involves observing and interpreting but no assessment. Statement B is descriptive but involves assessment. The teacher is saying that she (the teacher herself) knows that Liz knows how to pass the ball and will be able to do it again. The evidence for this assessment will be the perception of Liz's actions against the criteria of her intention and the result (did it match the intention?), and resemblance to basic technique. However, statement C gives a value, in this case 'very good' to a particular action on one occasion. Again, the criteria are taken for granted but would be the same as in statement B. On this occasion, either the technique or the effectiveness of the pass or both could be used as criteria for the assessment. But it does not say that Liz can pass the ball very well on other occasions, although she may very well be able to do so. 'Liz can pass the ball very well' which makes this implication is a different assessment, but applying the same criteria.

    As Broadfoot (1979) explains everybody continually makes judgments as part of everyday life and cannot avoid doing so, therefore it is not surprising that it goes on in schools. However, it is clear from the above examples that assessment is an essential and integral part of the teaching-learning situation, the essence of what schools are in business for. Teachers will make judgments continually as part and parcel of the teaching situation, and also may set up particular and formal assessment sessions, for example, tests and examinations to assess what the child can do and how well he or she can do it. In the educational context this 'how well' often takes the form of marks or grades, particularly in the formal testing situations. So Liz may receive a six out of ten or a 'C' for her passing in netball, and possibly the same mark or grade in the activity as a whole or in her GCSE. This is the public face of assessment. Many people recognize only the mark or grade as assessment or as worthwhile assessment, and many more see it as the most important part of it. Marks and grades are given so much prominence and status, not only because they are public knowledge, but because of the way they are used, for example, for selection purposes. A clear distinction needs to be made between what the marks or grades actually mean and their use. A mark or grade itself does not mean very much without reference to other pupils or a criterion, so we cannot actually say what Liz's six out of ten or C stands for. It only makes sense with knowledge of the assessment grade as a differentiating tool and as a standard of measure, and therefore we shall come back to this point under 'making sense of the judgment'. The purposes and uses as differentiating tools are more educational than technical, though they may dictate the technical, and will be discussed under other headings in chapter 2.

    It is at this point that I think it is necessary to distinguish between assessment and evaluation, two terms which have often been used synonymously because evaluation also means putting a value upon something. However, in educational circles evaluation is normally used in relation to programmes, curriculum, courses or teaching (though appraisal is now used in relation to the latter and to teachers), whereas, assessment is used in relation to pupils and students (Rowntree, 1977). Of course, there is a very close relationship between the assessment of students and the evaluation of programmes and the effectiveness of teaching and programmes, for example, the work of Carroll (1976a) on the evaluation of PE lessons shows that the overall evaluation of lessons is clearly determined by the assessment of the students in terms of attainment, behaviour and effort. However, in the American physical education literature the distinction between assessment and evaluation is not always observed, and here too there is a much closer link between assessment and testing and measurement.

The Basic Questions

Figure 1 shows the place of assessment in the teaching-learning context. The processes of perception, interpretation and judgment (PIJ) are not distinct phases but normally occur almost simultaneously in the teaching-learning episode. Both teachers and pupils undertake these processes, but it is only in recent years that teachers have consciously brought pupils more formally into the process through Records of Achievement and different teaching styles. This is the *who* of assessment (who does the assessing?).

There are two clear stages in the assessment process — in the *when* of assessment (when does assessment take place?). Firstly, the immediate within the interactive phase of the lesson, and secondly the post-lesson phase (Jackson, 1968; Carroll, 1976a). The most distinguishing features of the two phases in this time dimension are; in the first phase, the necessity for quick decisions and immediacy of action, and the ephemeral nature of the cues and evidence; in the second phase, the more considered reflection, and the overall impression from evidence 'lumped together' of practical work, and durable evidence in the form of written work. The latter can be particularly useful in assessing students over a long term and evaluating programmes as a more holistic view can be taken.

Teachers are, of course, assessing pupils, but it is the pupils' specific actions in a particular context which are the focal point of assessment. This is the *what* of assessment (what is assessed?). Thus PE teachers assess pupils in athletics, dance, games, gymnastics and other activities, and the pupils' knowledge about those activities and about the physical basis of performance (health related fitness programmes, GCSE) amongst other things using the broad dimensions of attainment, behaviour and effort as criteria (Carroll, 1976a; Veal, 1988). More specifically they use certain cues such as, particular movements, decisions taken, gestures, spoken or written words.

The way all this is done, such as observation and diagnosis, the modes of practices used to engage in the assessment process, (such as tests and examinations, and the setting up of practices to select the evidence), and the relation of criteria and cues to an ideal of what can be expected, are part of the *how* of assessment (how are the pupils assessed?).

Prior to all this are the intentions or purposes behind the assessment, such

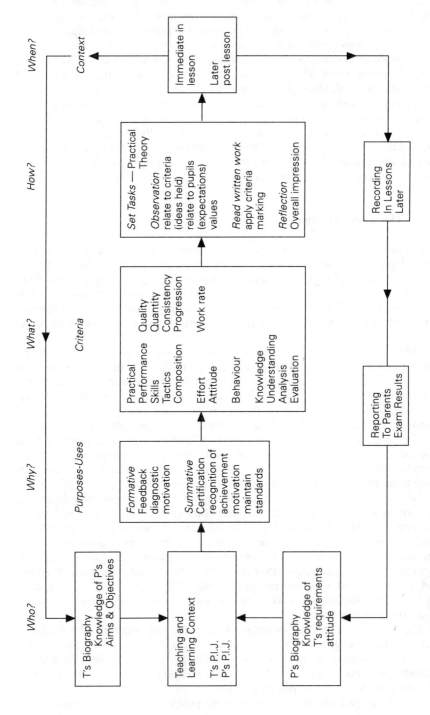

Figure 1: Model of assessment as part of the teaching-learning situation

Table 1: The key questions of assessment

Why assess?	Formative —	feedback diagnostic motivation
	Summative —	certification recognition of achievement motivation
Who is going to assess?		Teacher Pupil Both T+P, separately or negotiation
What will be assessed?		Knowledge and skills Personal qualities and attitudes Cross curricular themes Extra curricular activities Awards

How will it be assessed?

Through	*Context*	*Reference to*
Observation Experience Written	T-L situation Test situation	Criterion Group (norm) Self (ipsative)

How will it be recorded?	Format Grids Graded statements Banks of statements Use of Computer	Grades Marks

When will it be assessed?	In T-L situation Post lesson phase Other lessons Continuous, Periodic, Terminal	

as feedback or certification, and after the assessment is the use the assessment is put to, for example, selection. These are the *why* questions of assessment (why assess pupils? What use is made of it?).

The *why*, *who*, *what*, *when* and *how* are the key questions of assessment identified by most of the writers on assessment, and these questions will be discussed in later chapters in the context of PE. Table 1 summarizes these questions with general answers. The different answers to a given question should not be seen as distinct alternatives to each other as some can be used in conjunction with others.

Assessment is not only an integral part of teaching and learning, it should not be seen as a separate process even in the form of examinations and other summative assessments. It should be seen as part of a teaching-assessment-evaluation cycle, which at all points in the cycle feeds back information to both teacher and pupil for teaching purposes (formative assessment), to affect further action in the teaching-learning context and for curriculum and teaching evaluation (figure 2). Teachers and pupils have been put in the centre as they are at the heart of this process because they are continually influencing the cycle — it is

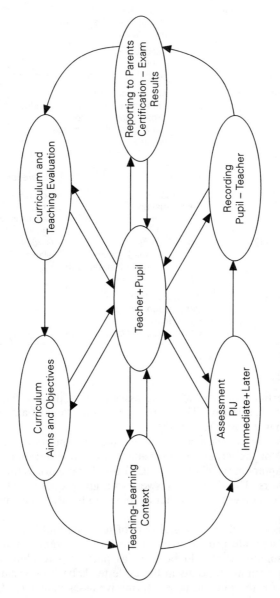

Figure 2: The teaching assessment — evaluation cycle

both a dynamic and dialectic relationship between assessor and those assessed whatever form it may take.

Making Sense of Assessment

Earlier we saw how a judgment was made of Liz's netball performance; it was made in relation to an ideal of techniques and skills which are known to be effective. What has happened here is that a comparison has been made with specific criteria, so we know whether Liz can do certain aspects of the game and play netball well or badly in relation to that criteria. But what do we make of the six out of ten and the overall C grade? What on earth do these values mean? They only make sense in relation to the particular criteria and assessment practices of the syllabus, so we can look at the GCSE syllabus to find out. In fact, a comparison is being made with a given standard. It is clear then that marks by themselves do not indicate very much, but they do when making comparisons either with the self, other people or groups, or a given standard, and these are known as ipsative, norm and criterion referencing respectively. I would like to illustrate the use of these assessments by a further example.

David is a 16-year-old and has received a nine out of ten for his technique and skills and an eight out of ten for his performance in the full game situation of badminton. On a ROA/report he receives an 'A' for attainment and an 'A' for effort. Peter is an 11-year-old working on a badminton module, and he has received ten for techniques and skills and nine for his matchplay and again received an 'A' for attainment and also for effort. Peter can beat all the pupils in his class, but in the extra curriculum club he plays David several times and always loses 15–0. How can Peter be awarded a higher mark? How can the teacher remark that Peter has done well against David and say that it was a good effort? This is easily explained by the fact that, although marks are given in relation to criteria in badminton, they are also given in relation to expectation of what pupils of a given age, development or experience can normally do. So, both David and Peter, in spite of the results of the match, are deemed worthy of these marks because they have been marked in relation to the group of which they are part. Peter's technique and play are good, exceptional, in fact, for his age, but he lacks the power, speed, court coverage and experience to be effective against David, who is five years older. If he had to be compared to David or David's age group, his mark for match play would be low. Peter would still be given an 'A' for effort in spite of being completely outplayed because he continued to run, and tried hard to reach the shuttle. Both Peter and David could compare their marks and grades, based on badminton criteria, with their own marks gained in previous or subsequent years and this would be useful to show progress and to relate to their own abilities.

What this example shows is that criterion referencing is not necessarily divorced from, or in conflict with, normative or ipsative referencing. It is being used in conjunction with it. Criteria and tasks are being used to differentiate pupils on degree of difficulty and outcome. These criteria and tasks are drawn up by teachers based on normative expectations of pupils' attainment, and therefore criterion referencing can mask a normative approach to differentiation, as in the GCSE.

Norm referencing has been the dominant comparison used in assessment in education until very recently. Its main purpose has been to compare performances within a group, whether that is the age, class, or year in the school or in society at large. As Satterly (1989) states, it shows,

> individual i exhibits more (or less) of characteristic x than the mean amount of y (the population). (p. 40)

PE teachers have been using this system on school reports for years when they have been using the five-point scale A–E for attainment and for effort. However, knowing where a child stands in relation to a particular group is not very useful and can be misleading if nothing is known about the group. Peter's 'A' grade on a five-point scale may well be justified in a weak group, but in other schools in the area, he may well find he is only average and would receive a 'C'. Pupils, too, use a norm referencing assessment a lot to compare their own performances and other pupils too. How often do we hear children saying 'I'm no good', or 'He's no good'. This is nearly always used with reference to other pupils rather than a criterion. This assessment is picked up through their own observation, of course, but the idea of comparison with others may be picked up through they way school teachers, family and adults convey their opinions and judgments.

We have heard much more about criterion referencing in recent years. Whereas the GCE and CSE were norm-referenced examinations, the GCSE, and now the National Curriculum key stage assessments, are criterion-referenced. As we have seen the purpose is to relate performance to a given standard, to test whether certain tasks can be mastered. PE teachers have used this a lot in everyday teaching, and in award schemes such as the Athletic Association's five-star award, where objective standards of time and distance are easily assessed. However, variable conditions, such as surfaces and weather, can make the criterion standards and the norms they are based on less than useful. As we have seen with David and Peter the application of the criteria is not always clear cut. The mastery of the technique and skills is open to subjective interpretation.

Ipsative referencing is most useful to record learning and progress. As the comparison is made with the pupil's previous performances then the starting point is immaterial. This type of referencing is central to child-centred philosophy and individual programmes, and can be the basis for self and teacher assessments in ROA. Although PE teachers will have used this form of comparison in formative assessment situations of teaching and learning, and for motivational purposes, it is perhaps at it strongest in activities such as educational gymnastics and dance where the child sets the criteria and the standards.

Although it is educationally useful to know how well a child is mastering certain skills (criterion referencing), and how much he or she is progressing (ipsative referencing), in the end comparisons with other children are inevitable in public grading systems, and in team performances and selection (normative referencing). Educational philosophies and policies are often conflated with political purposes and uses in assessment practices, as we have seen recently in National Curriculum assessments and examination results in the form of league tables.

Satterly (*ibid*) gives an excellent summary in table form of the differences between norm reference and criterion reference assessment. I am going to take this idea and use most of his categories, such as purposes, interpretation of scores, but add a few of my own, for example, ideology, uses, and also include self (ipsative) referencing which Satterly neglects (table 2). However, unlike Satterly, whose statements in each category are general, I am giving a specific example from PE in each method of referencing in each of the categories.

Mode of Assessment

Rowntree (1977) compiled a list of the most prevalent modes of assessment in education, and presented them as bipolar constructs. Satterly (1989) also uses this classification and there are excellent discussions in both these books. The modes are:

informal	versus	formal
continuous	"	terminal
process	"	product
convergent	"	divergent
formative	"	summative
coursework	"	examinations
internal	"	external
idiographic	"	nomothetic

As Satterly points out each dimension does not provide 'mutually exclusive alternatives' overall as any one school or any one course may use both ends of the dimension, for example, course work and examinations. Neither are these dimensions exclusive or alternative to each other, for example, examinations are a formal mode of assessment and often terminal too with external or internal examiners, and coursework may be continuously assessed by internal examiners and used formatively or be examined externally. They are not alternatives to each other because they are dealing with different aspects of assessment. Rowntree discusses them all in a chapter 'How to Assess', but in fact some of these dimensions answer the basic 'what', 'when', 'who' and 'why' questions of assessment as well as the 'how'. To be fair to Rowntree this is implicit in his discussions, but I want to emphasize that the distinctions are based on the key questions.

The following dimensions answer the *'how'* question: informal v. formal, coursework v. examinations, formative v. summative, ideographic v. nomethetic.

Informal v. formal states the *context* in which the assessment takes place, and describes the broad method. Formal usually refers to assessments that have been set up for that specific purpose, for example, written or practical tests for GCSE PE whilst informal refers to assessments which are not specifically set up for that purpose, but which take place as part of PE teaching situations.

Coursework v. examinations refers to a *method* of examining, but both of these may include different techniques, for example, notes, reports, essays, practical assessments, practical performances, seen and unseen papers. Coursework usually refers to anything that is done during or at the end of a course, but examinations refer to questioning or tasks set under prescribed conditions, such as the normal unseen paper with a set number of question for candidates to answer. Practical performance tasks can of course be set under examination conditions. It is possible that a series of tests under examination conditions could be demanded

Table 2: A Comparison of the 3 different reference systems using an example from PE

	Ipsative Reference	Norm Reference	Criterion Reference
Example	Pupil's educational gymnastics sequence of own creation.	Pupil's fitness test score.	Pupil's attempts at scoring a number of baskets from a set position.
Ideology	Child centred.	Group centred.	Activity centred.
Purpose	Comparison with pupil's own previous sequence. To assess progress.	Comparison with group fitness scores. To assess how fit pupil is in relation to other pupils of same age.	Comparison with a standard (scoring baskets). To assess how much skill pupil has mastered of scoring baskets from a set position.
Diagnostic	Whether pupil needs to work on the sequence and what part of the sequence.	Which pupils need remedial fitness work.	What needs remedial work. Whether scoring at baskets does.
Interpretation of Assessment/ Scores	How well or badly pupil has done in relation to previous sequences. Improving or not.	To see the relative position of pupil in the group in terms of fitness.	Indicates level of mastery of scoring baskets from set position.
Variations in Assessment/ Score	Other pupil's assessment not important. Pupil's own assessment important (i.e. self-assessment). Variation in own assessments indicate improvement or otherwise in sequence.	Need a range of scores amongst pupils on standardised set of scores.	Range of scores not important unless wishing to differentiate as in G.C.S.E. Depends on uses. Variation indicates different level of mastery of scoring.
Items in Assessment	Task difficulty related to what pupil can do.	Items related to the group to obtain norm or distribution. Number of items usually required.	Task difficulty not important. Related to specific criteria, e.g. scoring baskets from set position.
Role/Uses in Education	Value for own sake. What aspects of the sequence or go on to next sequence. Readiness. Motivation – self performance and progress. Accountability – self.	How fit a person is. Selection for sport/action. Fitness gradings. What aspects of fitness to work on. Motivation – other performance norms. Accountability – do better for group.	Selection based on mastery of skill, e.g. basketball team. Decide whether to go on to next skill or further practice required. Motivation – mastery of skills. Accountability –
Logical inference	Pupil shows a performance in a sequence which is better or worse than previous performances.	Pupil shows an amount of fitness which is greater or less than the mean of the tested for fitness.	Pupil shows an amount of mastery of scoring baskets which is greater or equal to criterion score.

for coursework, so these bipolar constructs are not necessarily opposites. Both methods are in use in GCSE PE.

Formative v. summative refers to the *context*, and describes its form in relation to purpose and use. In this respect it also answers the *'why'* question and partly the *'when'* question. It is not a method or technique. Formative refers to assessments which are used in the process of interaction to develop the person, such as in the teaching-learning situation in PE where diagnosis, feedback, correction or confirmation takes place. Summative is a more overall assessment, a summing up of a person's performances either over a specific course or courses, at a particular assessment such as in an examination grade. In practice there is not always a clear cut distinction between the two forms, as formative assessments can be used summatively, and summative statements can be used formatively at a later date. Both are prevalent in ROA.

Idiographic v. nomothetic: Rowntree (1977) makes the distinction between these two constructs as follows:

> This idiographic assessment aims to find out about an individual and arrive at a meaningful understanding of his uniqueness ... Nomothetic assessment, on the other hand, while it collects data about individuals, does so with a view to comparing one with another, generalizing from those assessed to others who have not been assessed, and aiming to understand people in general. (p. 158)

He goes on to relate idiographic to formative assessment and nomothetic to summative. What is surprising is that he does not relate them to ipsative and norm referencing respectively, because they clearly use the comparisons to self and groups. This dimension appears also to refer to how the assessment is used, and also answers the *'why'* question.

The following dimension answers the 'What' question.

Process v. product refers to *what* is being assessed. Definitions of the process end of the dimension are generally not very clear in most writings. Product is much easier to define and is something which is produced, such as a message in written work or a performance in the practical situation. Process is the ways and means the product is produced, not the techniques used but the actual experiences of doing something, such as observation, working, learning a skill, co-operation and making decisions. Here I am going to disagree with Rowntree when, in his example of drama, he says because the performance is not tangible, 'not 'out there', awaiting scrutiny', as an essay would be, it is a process. This example is akin to performances in the practical situation in PE. Rowntree is guilty of confusing product with process in this instance. The performance is the product, though there is the process of the act of performing. As most writers agree it is extremely difficult to actually assess process separately from the product. I am going to suggest that a teacher can observe a pupil 'processing', such as learning a skill, but can only infer the process of learning by assessing the product, the performance. If process is the actual experiences of doing something as suggested above, then, perhaps, the only satisfactory assessment of process is self-assessment. The teacher in this case may become a facilitator in this process.

Convergent v. divergent refers to a type of thinking (after Hudson, 1966) which is being assessed and is therefore a *'what'* question. Convergent refers to focusing on a clearly defined task with a single correct answer, but divergent refers to producing a wider variety of answers to a task. This does have parallels with performances in games situations, and open and closed type of skills in physical activities.

The two remaining dimensions answer two different basic questions, the *when* and *who* questions.

Continuous v. terminal refers to when the assessment takes place, and is a time dimension. Continuous means the pupil is being assessed throughout or at various intervals during the course, whilst terminal means at the end. Both are used in GCSE PE.

Internal v. external refers to the *control* of the assessment, and *who* is doing the assessing, whether it is within the school, or by an outsider, such as examination bodies. Internal may refer to pupils or teachers. It is quite common to have internal examiners or assessors, but have external moderation as in GCSE coursework. This means that the work is not being examined by the outsider, but the teacher's marks or grades are being compared to other teachers' marks or against criteria to check on the standard of marking. Both again are common in GCSE PE. This will clearly be referred to again in the more detailed discussions in the PE context in later chapters.

Principles of Assessment

We have now established what assessment actually is, how the teacher makes sense of the judgment, and the fundamental dimensions of assessment in the form of key questions — what, when, how, why and who. But these have not told us upon what basis the teacher selects the mode, method and technique to carry out the assessment, and upon what basis the assessment has taken place. Is Liz worth her six out of ten and overall 'C' grade? Has the teacher given a fair and appropriate judgment?

In order for the teacher to make a satisfactory and appropriate assessment, I am going to suggest that the teacher must adhere to what I am calling four fundamental principles, those of:

validity — including fitness for purpose and relevance.
reliability — consistency.
objectivity — free from bias.
clear criteria — according to what is assessed.

and consider and include as appropriate, what I am calling secondary principles;

variety of situations
balance of techniques
equality of opportunity

The assessment must also take into consideration the practical issues of time, work load for staff and pupils, and appropriate methods of recording.

Many teachers think that the four principles mentioned above apply only to tests, measurement and research methods, but they apply equally to other assessments as well. They are not some technical theoretical demand which has little relevance to the practical assessment situation. They are fundamental pre-requisites of fair, appropriate satisfactory assessments, as I hope to show in the following discussion.

Validity

In the technical literature different types of validity are identified (see Satterly, 1989), but they will only be mentioned where appropriate. Basically, validity is seeking to answer the question, 'does the assessment assess what it is supposed to assess?' (*construct validity*). To be worthwhile, the items or tasks set by the teacher must be related to the objectives, content and teaching methods used. In this respect, validity includes *fitness for purpose* and *relevance* to curriculum and pupils. Therefore it is not the items or task *per se* which are valid but their use and interpretation of them in relation to the purposes for which they were de-signed. So, if we return to Liz, who got a six out of ten for her netball passing, we can ask whether the task set actually allowed her the opportunity to show her netball passing and the teacher to assess it. We also need to know whether the objective was to see whether Liz could just pass the ball to another player accord-ing to an appropriate technique or whether she could produce the technical competence and effectiveness in a variety of game situations, or a combination of both. A situation could be set up where Liz is passing the ball to another player without opposition and outside a game situation just to see whether she can technically carry out the pass. Liz's six out of ten in this case, according to a given criteria, may well show she can pass with some degree of technical com-petence and accuracy. However, this may not be a valid test of her competence to carry out the skill in the game situation. It does not have *predictive validity* for the game. The complexity of the game situation and the pressure of the oppo-nents may reveal that she cannot pass technically or effectively as she did in the artificial situation outside the game, and in this case she is not worth a six out of ten. If the purpose was to assess her passing in the game of netball, then clearly the first task is not a valid one. This may seem very obvious, but the example does raise the question of what a teacher should assess and give marks for, which is something which has had to be tackled in GCSE PE. For example, Liz would have to answer in written form, questions on the rules/laws of netball and tech-niques and tactics if she took the GCSE under one examination board but not under another. In this other examination she would be 'assessed in the practical performance context'. Which is valid then? The validity of the written tests and answers may well be questionable in relation to practical performance in the actual game. Clearly this is something which will be returned to later. It should be noted that when assessments appear to assess something then this is known as *face validity*. However, face validity of a task does not mean that a task has construct validity. It is possible for a task to appear valid (has face validity) but is actually not valid (lacks construct validity). An example of this is when pupils' knowledge of the laws is assessed through officiating a game. The act of officiat-ing is more than knowledge of laws, it is also about decision-making in a particu-lar context.

Reliability

Basically, reliability refers to the consistency of the assessment, that is, in the circumstances, would the teacher give the same assessment on another occasion or, would other teachers give the same assessment? There is clearly a link with validity, but it is possible to have valid assessment, which is not always reliable, for example, essays and assessments of practical performance in games situations can fall into this category. It is also possible to have reliable assessments which are not valid for given criteria, such as, objective tests of games skills as a test of performance in the full game context.

Rowntree (1977) discusses some well known research which shows the low reliability of some assessments. Examination boards are, of course, well aware of the problems and try to overcome them by having standardising meetings for teachers and examiners, second markers, and moderation etc. Satterly (1989) treats the topic in a technical way showing how the reliability of assessment scores can be checked, and suggests the traditional methods, such as, test-retest, and split half testing, which are appropriate to formal testing situations only.

There was a lot of concern about the assessment of practical work, particularly in games and open skills context, and statements such as the Secondary Schools Examination Council that PE could not be assessed satisfactorily were widely believed (SSEC, 1963). This concern was really about the validity and reliability of the assessment. It was often thought that PE teachers would not be able to agree on the same mark, or how on they would mark the different aspects of the game, techniques, tactics, positioning, creativity, influence and contribution of the opposition and team members, and effort. This was usually because the criteria were not stated explicitly, and assessment assumed to be merely impressionistic. It has been shown through the GCSE that when criteria is made explicit, then assessment is reduced to much more of a technical exercise, which is open to standardization and moderation. My observation of GCSE standardization sessions suggests that there is a lot of basic agreement between teachers on the criteria and marks awarded.

Objectivity

Objectivity is the extent to which an assessment is free from personal bias. Clearly it has links with reliability, as a truly objective test will be reliable, for example, one based on measurement of time, distance or goals scored. Factual recall is also an objective assessment. However, much of what goes on in PE does not lend itself to purely objective assessment. So I am not advocating that all assessments must be objective in this sense. The assessment will be based on what is known as subjective interpretations and judgments by the teachers. What I am advocating is the attempt, as far as possible, by the teacher to free him/herself from personal biases, opinions etc. in applying criteria, assessment procedures and judgments. According to Best (1974), even artistic appreciation can be objective, and clearly this type of argument can be applied equally to all PE activities, not only dance. This will be returned to in later chapters.

Clear Criteria

It may seem obvious that teachers must have a set of clear criteria in mind in order to make satisfactory assessments. However, the lack of explicit criteria was common in PE and led to the idea that vagueness and general impression was all that could be achieved, particularly in games. GCSE has shown this to be false. It is not necessary to go into this in further detail here as it will be covered in detail in chapters 3 and 4.

At this stage it is not necessary to discuss what I have termed secondary principles, but they will clearly appear later when discussing the more detailed context of PE. At this stage it is only necessary to note that they should be applied to the assessment as appropriate. They clearly will not necessarily apply to every single assessment as do the four fundamental principles. It should be also noted here that it is no good applying all the principles if the result is that the assessments cannot be done in the limits of time and workload, or they effect the teaching situation or other children to such an extent that their overall education or learning is suffering. This has been one of the problems with the introduction of the National Curriculum assessments at key stage 1. Assessments must fit in with the practical situation of teaching and school organization, but at the same time, fundamental principles must not be sacrificed for time otherwise the assessment may not be worthwhile at all. What is clear from the problems raised by National Curriculum assessments at key stage 1, is that the basic purposes of the assessment need to be sorted out. In this instance there have been conflicting interests, and this has a lesson for everyone, including PE teachers.

It is a central tenet of this book that it is essential for teachers to sort out their purposes in the first instance, and these will then guide the practice and the methods of assessing and recording. Assessment will then become an integral part of the curriculum and the teaching-learning context and not some separate chore.

Chapter 2

Why Assess in Physical Education?

There are two basic questions to be answered in this chapter under the 'why' question. Firstly, what are the purposes and uses of assessment in PE? This is the fundamental question of 'why assess at all?' and the answers will have a lot in common with other subjects. But these purposes always existed, so, secondly, why did PE became involved in the formal assessment system such as examinations only in recent years and after it was generally and invariably thought as unnecessary and undesirable to do so? I will deal with the second question first.

Why PE Became Involved in Formal Assessment

Until recently, and in contrast to other major subjects on the curriculum, physical education in schools had been characterized generally by a lack of formal assessment. This is not to say that informal or formal assessment had not taken place, and as we have seen, informal assessment is an integral part of teaching and learning. The main forms of assessment in PE were:

(i) comments on the now much maligned school report. Teachers often had to make their comments under pressure of time and limitations of space. The comments were often short, general or vague, such as 'satisfactory' meaning either 'the pupil is satisfactory' or 'I am not sure who he/she is, so must be satisfactory', but often did make reference to the central dimensions of attainment or ability and effort (Carroll, 1980). It was common to give a grading on a five-point scale of A to E (normative) on the dimensions of attainment and effort. PE teachers usually made it difficult for themselves and in particular to make accurate assessments as they did not normally have recorded evidence of attainments. The purpose of the report was to give information about the pupils to their parents, but they were not always treated too seriously and the value placed on them by teachers, pupils and parents was inconsistent and open to question. Teachers who had to take a large number of classes and pupils had difficulty knowing all the pupils in any detail. However, reports were generally manageable. These have been superseded by Records of Achievement which will be looked at in more detail later;

(ii)   assessment for National Governing Body Award Schemes. This was probably the most formal, accurate and recorded assessment made by PE teachers, but the extent to which they were used is not known. Schemes such as the Amateur Athletics Association (AAA) five-star award and the Amateur Swimming Association (ASA) used objective measures of time and distance, whilst the British Gymnastics Association (BAGA) awards, which were very popular with the primary schools, listed specific gymnastic skills to be achieved.

It is interesting to note that, in the light of modern developments in education (for example, GCSE, National Curriculum), all these were criterion reference awards, though of course the times and distances were based on norms for a specific population (normative). The purpose of these was to give certification, and was essentially motivational.

(iii) assessment for the selection of school teams. The provision of school teams and extra curricular competition were normally regarded as one of the main functions of the PE teacher (see Glew, 1983). The assessment itself could be regarded as informal but the selection was made formal and public by the fact that anyone could see who was selected. Teams were often put on the noticeboard. It was a normative system, and selection depended very much on the strength (numbers and ability) of a particular group at any given time and the perceptions of teachers. Normally the interests of the school or team came before the interests of individual pupils or equality of opportunity. Apart from the selection of individuals and development of individual talent, the purpose of school teams lay in school publicity and public relations, and a yardstick to assess the PE teachers' commitment and coaching ability.

The main features of these assessments, unlike most other subjects, have been the ephemeral and fleeting evidence, the lack of specific criteria except in award schemes, the lack of systematic observation and recording and the reliance on general impressions (Carroll, 1976a and 1980). The consequences of these factors were that, until the mid-1970s, assessment had not been seen as an important issue in physical education. Serious discussion on the purposes, issues and problems had rarely taken place, and assessment had not been treated as problematic in either teacher training or research.

PE in the fourth to fifth years began to change from the beginning of the 1970s after the first entries into CSE mode III courses with the Southern Regional Examination Board. At first the uptake was very slow, but the pace quickened with the arrival of mode I courses in the Southern and West Midlands regions, and again with the introduction of the GCSE in 1986 (see Carroll, 1982, 1986a, and 1990a; Schools Council, 1977 and 1981 for the development). Table 3 shows the rise in the number of schools and pupils for CSE and GCSE PE. It is perhaps not surprising that PE took some time to become accepted as an examination subject when one considers that those in favour were fighting, and they had to fight hard, against a long tradition and against very influential organizations, for

Table 3: Number of centres and candidates for CSE and GCSE in selected years

Syllabus	Year	Centres	Candidates
CSE PE	1978	395	7,513
CSE PE	1985	643	13,109
Dance		214	2,896
OP		59	683
GCSE PE 1	1988	N.K.	18,831
GCSE PE 1	1990	N.K.	34,529
GCSE PE 1	1992	N.K.	43,436*
PE 2/3			598
Dance			2,754
OP			137

* includes 922 NISEAC, and 486 MEG Sport Studies (see table 16).

example, the Secondary Schools Examination Council (SSEC) (1963) and the Schools Council (1977), and against influential individuals (for example, Evans, 1976; Woollam, 1978; Hargreaves, 1982). Many of the examination boards used the SSEC's 1963 statement to discourage the submission of syllabuses. It is worth looking at the main points of the SSEC's statement (1963) as they were so instrumental in the formation of examination boards' policies and in holding back development, but they are too detailed to repeat in full here. The main points were:

The difficulty of assessing qualitative aspects of movement and games, and lack of objectivity except in athletics and swimming (times, distances).

The most significant aspect of PE cannot be measured validly (but doesn't say what these are).

The difficulty of comparing activities.

The difficulty of assessing all aspects of the programme.

Differences in individual development (physique, temperament) — no common starting point.

Difficulty of seeing the purpose or value, its own intrinsic motivation, doesn't need the stimulus.

In 1977 the Schools Council PE Committee repeated the full SSEC Statement and added a few of their own (Schools Council, 1977). Most of those arguments lacked substance and evidence, and in the light of CSE and GCSE can be seen to be invalid. The Schools Council began to change its recommendations under pressure of the development of CSE (Schools Council, 1981).

The situation began to change from the early 1970s when the first mode III CSE PE courses began to appear. In spite of the very strong opposition, the interest in examinations grew steadily during the CSE years, but with renewed impetus at the introduction of GCSE (see table 3). Carroll (1986a) identifies four phases in the development of examinations.

(i) Early 1970s — gaining acceptance, getting established, ironing out difficulties, specific regions, modes III's (own syllabuses).
(ii) Mid/late 1970s — rapid expansion, extension to all regions.
(iii) Early 1980s — introduction of mode I's (boards' syllabuses), consolidation.
(iv) Mid/late 1980s — introduction of GCSE and rapid expansion, introduction of A levels.

It was certainly a story of 'grass roots development' which may account for its success and it was certainly a fight against tradition. Sparkes (1991a) has indicated the difficulty of making changes and innovations within a department, but the development of examinations entailed persuading public bodies, the examination boards, to change their policies. So why did it happen? As Broadfoot (1979) has shown assessment is a product of prevailing ideologies and conditions at the time. Therefore we must look at the nature of PE in the late 1960s and early 1970s, and also to educational ideologies of the time. It is a case of linking teachers' perceptions and actions to more structural changes and the evidence and the argument is based on Carroll's research (Schools Council, 1981; Carroll, 1982).

The main thrust of the curriculum in the upper secondary school in the 1960/70s was recreational with the emphasis on games and education for leisure (see Kane, 1974). Whether the school programme was wide with the opportunity to take options and very often in activities not covered in the lower secondary school, or narrow due to limitations of facilities, staff and tradition, the emphasis was on playing the game. Generally there was not a lot of specific teaching going on. Extra-curricular activities and inter-school sport was usually regarded as just as important a part of the PE teachers' job as the curriculum teaching, and often received more attention from headteachers, governors and other staff and was a way the PE teacher could make his/her name, and gain prestige.

However the thrust in education was changing. The introduction of CSE, and comprehensive education shifted the focus of educational debate from 11+ to 16+ examinations and brought more pupils into the examination system at 16. The practical subjects had always been awarded low status (Musgrove and Taylor, 1969) and regarded as marginal to the main functions of the school, though they were also regarded as having a strong supporting role in the socialization role (Hendry, 1975; Mangan, 1973; Carroll, 1982). The changes brought less support from other staff in terms of time in curriculum time and extra-curricular activities, a threat to non-examination subjects, and a threat to PE for brighter pupils (they didn't have the time for PE). PE teachers felt the effects of their low status and marginal role. At the same time many PE teachers found it difficult to move jobs for promotion or sideways into other subjects. In the past many PE teachers had changed jobs in their thirties or forties to go into advising, lecturing, counselling, primary or more classroom-based jobs, but many of those avenues were drying up due to LEA or government policies, so now teachers were having to stay in their PE post for longer periods of time. Many of these teachers needed a stimulus, challenge and professional development and the CSE gave them this opportunity.

Many teachers too were dissatisfied with their role as recreationalists. Education for leisure was long-term, vague and marginal and failed to be encaptured by a whole-school policy and it was difficult to say how successful it was. The option system had created some interest for both teachers and pupils but often depressed standards and failed to get beyond the low level. CSE gave a real sense of purpose and motivation for pupils and teachers which the recreation programme lacked. The teachers looked for justification in CSE and health schemes. So, although the innovation of CSE was legitimized on sound educational grounds as one would expect and related to pupil objectives of gaining knowledge and understanding, studying in depth motivation and certification, it was also a mechanism for compensation for role dissatisfaction, role survival, professional development, and status redefinition. It brought PE into a more central role, part of the the selective mechanisms and allocative functions of the school. Table 4 summarizes the changes in direction of fourth and fifth year PE on the introduction of examinations in PE in schools and colleges.

The early development can now be seen to be extremely important in the examination story for they led to the introduction of mode I in certain regions (Southern, West Midlands, Southeastern, East Anglia,) which, in turn, led to its acceptance in the more prestigious GCSE examination on its introduction in 1986. The development of CSE mode I's and GCSE renewed impetus to the examination development as they allowed teachers to enter the examination system without having to initiate and develop their own syllabuses, which was time consuming and not without difficulties and unease for the teachers. The examination innovation could be said to move from the individual level model to the institutional level.

There were probably two other events which were significant and gave an impetus to thinking about the curriculum and thereby the examinations. Firstly, the teachers' strike about pay and conditions of service in the mid-1980s resulted in a decline in extra curricular activities. Secondly the attack on competition, which affected extra curricular inter school sport (Glew, 1983; Pollard, 1988). This also brought a decline in extra-curricular activities and in particular inter-school sport. Although, of course, these have continued in many forms and in many activities in recent years there has been less emphasis on this aspect of the teachers' role. This has allowed a greater focus on the curriculum. The GCSE was arguably the most important educational issue and development in the mid-1980s and so many PE teachers looked at it along with their colleagues from other subjects in a new light for many of the reasons stated above.

PE's involvement in Records of Achievement (ROA) and the National Curriculum are much more straightforward. More details of the development of ROA are given in chapter 7. Although again, in ROA-like examinations, there were many individual developments, pilot schools often produced whole school policies or involved all subjects. Many PE teachers saw this as an opportunity to record pupils' achievements which had been neglected on the former school report and were valued by many pupils, parents and employers. Some PE teachers took a central role in the development of PE ROA and in the school, for example, Skinsley (1986), and Hatfield and Phillips (1989). In spite of the difficulties for PE teachers, particularly related to time and organization, the value of ROA as a motivational force and as a measure of accountability was noted and teachers were keen to spread their ideas (see Bulletin of PE, 1986; BJPE, 1989; and

Table 4: *Changes in direction on the introduction of examinations in PE departments in schools and colleges[1]*

Changes in	Pre Examination	CSE, GCSE, 'A' level	C&G, BTEC
Ideological base	Recreational	Educational	Vocational
Knowledge	Practical (knowing how, physical experience) Narrow (activity related)	Practical and theoretical (how and what) Broad (activity related plus sciences and social sciences.)	Theoretical (how and what) Broad — employment related (Recreation & Leisure industries)
Assessment criteria	Participation in physical activities Performance — school and club teams.	Performance level in physical activities. Theoretical knowledge and understanding. Examination results.	Performance — academic and vocational. Examination results
Role of teacher	Recreationalist. Official. Supervisor. Organizer. Extra-curricular coach.	Educationalist. Teacher. Coach. Assessor. Examiner.	Educationalist. Vocational trainer. Assessor. Examiner.
Status	Marginal	Central	Central
Function	Supporting value system	Transmitting knowledge, skills, values. Supporting assessment system. Selective mechanism. Allocative.	Vocational training. Transmitter knowledge, skills, values. Selective mechanism, Economic. Allocative.

1 Adapted from Carroll, 1990.

chapter 7). Many more teachers have of course become involved since ROA became government policy.

PE's involvement in the National Curriculum is also of course through Government policy as PE was declared a foundation subject (DES, 1989b). However, PE, along with art and music, has been treated differently from the other foundation subjects especially in relation to assessment. The details of this will be discussed in chapter 8. The recognition of PE as a foundation subject does accept PE's centrality in the curriculum and functioning of the school. However, its different treatment again leaves questions over its status and reduces the effectiveness and value of its assessment. The crucial question of the detailed relationship of the National Curriculum to GCSE and ROA have yet to be determined and are relevant to this issue (see chapter 8).

Becoming an examination subject and an essential part of ROA and the National Curriculum has meant that PE has become more centrally involved in the functions of the school moving from a more marginal role to a more central one (see Hendry, 1975; and table 4). However, it has also meant involvement in the ideologies of assessment, and has meant sacrificing some freedom, accepting external control and different roles in return for more clarity of role, personal development and satisfaction (in spite of general low morale often cited) and possibly even survival.

Now we come to the fundamental question of the purposes of assessment.

The Purposes of Assessment

It is endemic in education that the idea of formal assessment, in particular examinations, remains unquestioned and unproblematic. It is part of the 'taken for granted' aspect of schooling and the education system. As Broadfoot (1979) suggests:

> The prevailing ideology of assessment is such that its central tenets are not seen as problematic. That it is both necessary and desirable for teachers and external examiners (but seldom the pupils themselves) to grade pupils according to certain kinds of performance (usually academic), in particular groupings of knowledge (some of higher status than others), usually in some kind of rank order, and on the basis to select some for opportunities leading to prestigious positions and usually high material rewards, and to reject others (i.e. the majority) for occupational roles of little reward and influence, is largely taken for granted by both experts and the general public.

This clearly indicates the most important function of the school and the central part that assessment plays in this function. Broadfoot is clearly referring to a societal selection purpose, but, of course, there are other purposes too at the classroom level, which contribute to this overall purpose as well as being useful at this more specific classroom level such as feedback and diagnosis. PE, as I have already pointed out, has always included some aspects of assessment, particularly informal assessment, but it has now entered the formal assessment arena with certification — selection purposes as its central tenet. If we look at the way

Table 5: The main purposes of assessment as identified by selected authors

Broadfoot (1979)	Rowntree (1977)	Satterly (1989)	Gipps (1990)
Accountability	Maintain standards	Accountability	Control
Certification	Selection	Certification	Certification
Motivation	Motivation	Goal setting	Selection
Diagnosis	Feedback	Diagnosis	Diagnosis
	Preparation for life	Feedback	Screening

purposes have been categorized we can see that they cover the two levels — societal and classroom. Gipps (1990) refers to these two levels of assessment as professional, where it is used to help the teacher in the process of educating the child, and managerial, where results help manage the education system.

It is not always easy to distinguish between purposes and uses, and there is sometimes an overlap between purposes. They are not discrete categories, for example, certification can be used for selection and motivation.

The main purposes of assessment have been discussed under various headings by different authors. These are summarized in table 5. The main categories selected for discussion in relation to PE are those common to most of the authors. Table 6 shows these main purposes of assessment related to level, form of assessment, characteristics and uses or the way they functioning.

Accountability

This is the most general of the purposes and is at two levels. Firstly, societal (managerial) which is about maintenance of overall standards, control and value for money. It poses the question, 'Are schools and teachers doing a good job?' Secondly, at a more interpersonal level in the classroom (professional), it is about accountability to parents and pupils, and the performances, behaviour and needs of individual pupils.

Societal Level (Managerial)

There are frequent periodic crises of confidence and 'moral panic' (Cohen, 1972) over educational standards, for example, the impact of James Callaghan's Ruskin speech, Cox and Dyson's *Black Papers* in the mid-1970s. The most current of these have been the Government's attacks, firstly, on primary schools' standards of reading and writing after the publication of the National Curriculum test results when the blame was put on teaching styles and teacher training, and, secondly, on the reliability of GCSE standards. Standards are often said to be falling, but the evidence for direct comparisons and to support the criticism is not always available to substantiate the claims. The simple use of examination results or National Curriculum tests is full of pitfalls and fails to consider pupils' ability and background and the standardization procedures or lack of them. But what we have seen lately through National Curriculum tests and examination results is an attempt to control the curriculum by the Government and to make comparisons

Table 6: Purposes of assessment related to levels, forms, functions and characteristics

Purpose	Level		Forms	Functions Characteristics
Accountability of teachers and schools	Professional	To Parents, Pupils, Headteacher, Governors	Informal, Tests, Exams ROA, Reports NC ES	Individual needs, Performance, standards T. motivation
Accountability of teachers and schools	Managerial	To LEA, Government, Employers	NC testing, Exams Publication of Results Fitness, Activity levels	Economic, spending Educated workers Overall standards T. motivation
Certification of pupils	Professional Managerial	By School, LEA, Exam Bodies, Governing Bodies of Sport	ROA GCSE, 'A' level BTEC, Award schemes	For achievement Selection, Vocational training P. motivation
Feedback to pupils	Professional	By Teachers	Direct to P. after informal assessment and tests, exams	Formative P. learning, behaviour motivation
Diagnosis of pupils	Professional	By Teachers, Specialists	Observation Testing	P. strengths and weaknesses, Screening, Selection
Motivation of pupils	Professional	By Teachers	Informal assessment Testing, Certification	P. performance, behaviour, attitude, effort
Selection for school teams	Professional	By Teachers, Other pupils	Informal Formal	Standards P. motivation and performance

between schools and LEAs. It is being used to answer the question, both crudely and unfairly, 'Whose doing a good job and giving value for money?' It has enabled the Government to blame LEAs and cutback on their spending, to criticize teaching standards and styles and teacher training without real justification, and to attack examination boards without hard evidence.

Although at the primary level the debate mainly focuses on the 3Rs and the National Curriculum core subjects (at present — key stage 1) and at secondary level on the key stage 3 pilot tests in selected subjects and the GCSE results, PE is not immune from the effects of this debate. In those subjects not at the centre of debate and not in the examination or assessment system, teachers will find they do not have to be as accountable, but the pressure comes in a squeeze on their time and on a rationale for being in the curriculum. As we have seen, PE had faced this problem to a certain extent at 15+ and 16+ and met it by entering the CSE and GCSE system. Its entry into the National Curriculum had perhaps assured its place in the curriculum, but its late entry and its different treatment will also ensure it receives a lower status and therefore less time and resources. Its entry into GCSE means it will be included in publicized school league tables, and the pressure to get good results, select the best pupils to enter the examination, to focus more narrowly on the important assessment component will be strong. Increasingly it looks as if accountability through the National Curriculum testing at the end of key stages and examination results (GCSE at 16+) will become more important. The government is telling the public that tests and examination results are the most important criteria for judging schools performance, standards of educational achievement, showing money is well spent, and selecting a school for their children in the market economy approach. It is difficult for PE to compete with these criteria and pressures on the social, leisure or health front, although a school may wish to give publicity to these objectives and to PE programmes, sports and physical extra curricular activities as support in the marketing of the school.

The quality control over progression through the statutory National Curriculum testing on ten levels within explicit attainment targets does not exist in PE. The statements at the four Key Stages will not necessarily help to maintain standards but will lead to vagueness in assessment. It is going to be impossible to use the National Curriculum assessments in PE for comparison between schools or to show standards (see chapter 8). However, GCSE PE results may certainly be used in this way.

The debates on standards have not totally bypassed PE. Recently there has been a concern about the standards of, and decline in, the amount of school sport, and decline in standards of fitness and health, Pollard (1988) suggests that it did reach the proportions of 'moral panic' It did have media coverage and was debated in Parliament (see *Panorama* TV programme, 1987; Pollard, 1988; School Sport Forum, 1988; SHA Survey, 1990; ITV, 1992). In a rather muddled argument which conflated the aims of PE with the aims of sport and the decline of standards of fitness brought about by changing lifestyles, Panorama presented an attack on school PE and sport, particularly the new anti-competitive PE. Although there is evidence of a decline in extra curricular sport (SHA Survey, 1990), there is no evidence of a decline in national standards of sport. The changing relationship between PE and sport has been overshadowed by the ERA (Murdoch, 1990) but there are now closer links which will continue to maintain the standard of participation in sport. The National Curriculum will ensure that pupils start from a wide base of six activity groupings in the primary years to end of key stage 2 and at least four activities until the age of 14 (key stage 3), instead of the common practice of a narrower base in the early years leading to a wide number of options beyond age 14. The National Curriculum proposals take a wide view of performance with its demands of an evaluation component of performance, the different roles such as officiating and knowledge of community participation and a built-in health focus.

There is rightly concern for childrens' physical fitness and activity levels and the need to encourage more exercise (Fentem, Bassey and Turnbull, 1988), and Armstrong (1990) links lack of activity with coronary heart disease (CHD). However, Armstrong (1987) warns of the dangers and inadequacies of fitness tests and the use of norms based on age for use in schools. The School Sport Forum (1988) advocated a daily session of physical activity and although this could have the right effect and form the habit of regular physical activity it could also possibly turn some children off exercise if not handled correctly. However, it must be borne in mind that PE is not only about improving the fitness levels of pupils, it has other aims and objectives, so time must be given also to achieving those objectives (see chapter 3). Nor would it be fair to just rely on PE lessons or to make PE solely responsible for the fitness of the nation especially in view of modern day lifestyles. PE has therefore tackled the fitness problem, in more recent years, by including health related fitness / activity programmes which place the emphasis on knowledge about fitness activity and its relation to health. This includes knowledge of fitness testing and on leading active lifestyles rather than getting the pupil fit *per se*.

There have been a number of major initiatives with a health focus in recent years such as the joint Health Education Authority (HEA) and Physical Education Association (PEA) project based at Loughborough University and the Happy Heart Project for primary school children based at the University of Hull (see Harris, 1988; Sleap, 1990) which have had a tremendous effect on teacher pro-grammes though the effect on children is not clear (see Jones, 1990). The National Curriculum proposals (DES, 1991b) surprisingly neglected the health focus in its rationale for PE and failed to include health programmes as separate pro-grammes of study. They appeared to offer a health focus as a 'permeation' model within activity-based programmes of study. It is doubtful whether this will be satisfactory as I suspect that a 'permeation' model can often lead to what I call an 'incidental' model, that is one where it is included incidentally and lacks the required focus. However, the proposals did take up the challenge by including statements at the end of the key stages.The National Curriculum should raise standards particularly in the primary schools and provide the basis for account-ability. However, the National Curriculum is marred by lack of guidance on assessment and it will need a massive in-service training programme to make effective (see chapter 8).

Classroom Level (Professional)

Teachers are, of course, accountable to their headteachers, who are ultimately responsible for what goes on in their schools. However, in the past head teachers normally treated their staff as professionals, expected them to be able to get on with the job and rarely visited classrooms, and even less likely the gym or playing fields, or demanded to see syllabuses. The head knew little about what went on in PE, thought of it as recreation which it often was in the upper secondary school, and as long as nothing went wrong organization or discipline-wise, then there was no interference, or quality control. PE teachers in primary and secondary schools were judged on their discipline, organization and on school team results and width of programmes. PE teachers, in the past, often got promotion or other jobs on the strength of their work in extra-curricular activities in school teams. In recent years this criteria has declined with the decline in school sport and an increasing focus on the curriculum. Clearly, GCSE results and possibly the number of pupils opting for the GCSE PE will replace those criteria in career moves. The ability to fulfil the National Curriculum requirements effectively will be used in the future for all subjects. However, the means of doing this in other subjects is the National Curriculum Attainment Target Levels which are not statutory in PE, and the end of key stage statements in PE are not precise enough (except for 25-yard swim) for this use. Pupils' GCSE results and ROA can be used indirectly by headteachers to see if the teachers are doing a good job. However, it is likely that the headteacher will rely on appraisal schemes and heads of departments for quality control in the subject area which will be part of a whole school policy on assessment. The organization of events such as sports days, extra curricular activities and inter-school sport are still good public relations for PE and the school and may still be partly used by headteachers, when it suits him/her in the market place approach. Accountability to the headteacher may well be on a wider front than in most other subjects. There is a parallel here with music and art, where teachers may well put on festivals, concerts, exhibitions on other public displays. This may still be necessary with the lower status accorded to these practical subjects in the National Curriculum.

I am not sure how far teachers have thought themselves accountable to pupils, or took seriously their accountability to parents. They fulfilled their accountability to parents through an annual parents evening, often the only time parents came to or were allowed in the school, and through the generally acknowledged inadequate school report. Reports have been replaced, and in primary schools are still being replaced, by ROA which are more detailed and useful, particularly for PE teachers. In recent years too the school has become more accessible, parents made more welcome and there is a closer liaison with parents and in many cases with the community. The school is now a 'marketable commodity' and information about what goes on is available in publicity material. This is an opportunity for PE teachers to show 'their wares', the rationale for their curriculum and market themselves. This approach is also political and it may be necessary to show that there are other aspects to the school, other needs beside as examination results. We must encourage active lifestyles. Accountability in PE is on a wide front, and is a powerful motivational force for teachers.

Certification

The most public purpose of education is certification, and because of this it is usually seen to be the most important, GCSE (and before that the CSE and GCE

'O' level) and 'A' levels are the most prominent. Their prominence and importance comes from the way they are used as selective mechanisms for employment and entry into higher education. In spite of the inadequacies of the assessment and the instruments (for example unseen examinations) and criteria for assessment (subject performance related, academic ability) in relation to the use and selection (for prediction of success in certain occupations), examinations and certification have persisted. Certification is seen as the epitome of the meritocratic society (Broadfoot, 1979), the objective evidence of merit in a differentiated society, and reward for work and level of performance. The classical and liberal theories of education for its own sake with intrinsic rewards, are insufficient for the functional, compulsory educational system and extrinsically driven society of today. Certification gives education and schooling its purpose and credibility, but it also serves to preserve inequalities and acts as a rejection system (Rowntree, 1977, Broadfoot, 1979). The 11+ examination was one of the best examples of this and that was why it came under attack.

As we have seen PE's entry into the formal examination system (CSE, GCSE, 'A' levels) was legitimated on educational grounds of furthering students' knowledge and understanding (see objectives of the syllabuses) and to gain a qualification (see Carroll, 1982, 1990a and 1991; Francis, 1990). Thus, the GCSE and 'A' level qualifications in the subject are now used as a means to gain entry to further and higher education, such as to 'A' level courses, BTEC courses in leisure studies, to degree courses in recreational management, and to enter employment such as in the armed forces, public services, professional sport administration. As career opportunities in recent years have widened considerably in the sporting and leisure industries the qualifications have been and will continue to be increasingly used as a basis for selection in these spheres.

However, the idea of certification and its use as a motivational force is not new in PE. As mentioned already, the governing bodies of sport award schemes have been frequently used in this way and pupils proudly wear the badges as evidence of their success. Sometimes the results have helped teachers select teams, particularly in Athletics. They have also given the teacher, especially the non specialist in junior schools an aim and structure to their lesson, for example the BAGA awards. However, they have also been known to dominate that part of the curriculum and have a detrimental effect on the learning of the children, focusing on the testing instead of on the teaching of the skills.

Feedback

By feedback I am referring only to the classroom level, as the more general level of overall results has been dealt with under accountability. This is where assessment is an integral part of teaching and learning and feedback is used to show the pupil how he/she is doing, learning and progressing. It is used by the teacher to see whether teaching points have been learnt and whether to move on to the next point. From the teachers point of view feedback is the most central and important purpose of formative assessment but usually gets the least public attention.

In PE where the emphasis is on physical skills and practical performance, it is essential for the pupil to know the results and effectiveness of techniques and skills, often in the immediate situation, so times and distances are given in athletics and in swimming, technical and tactical points are made in games skills, and technical and compositional advice given in gymnastics and dance. The pupil can then work at the skill and can set him/herself targets, compare with previous performances, and the teacher can evaluate his teaching and work (Carroll, 1976a and 1980). It is motivational for both pupil and teacher.

Diagnosis

Diagnostic assessment is the formal identification of strengths and weaknesses, and is usually done for correction purposes. Hence it is usually carried out in relation to children with special needs and often by educational psychologists or specialists. The more common reference to diagnosis in the analysis and correction of techniques is included under the concept feedback. Here it is used in a more clinical sense.

In PE, diagnostic assessment has been used to assess movement problems (Sugden, 1991) and with the mainstreaming of special needs pupils after Warnock (see Meek, 1991) there are more pupils with special needs in PE than previously. PE teachers need to be acutely aware of their difficulties and needs. The advent of the National Curriculum would suggest that special consideration will have to be given to these children (see DES, 1991b) and perhaps more diagnostic facilities or training for PE teachers need to be available.

The diagnosis of physical fitness needs has long been a use of fitness tests (see Bosco and Gustafson, 1983). The concern expressed about childrens' fitness levels (Fentem, Bassey and Turnbull, 1988; Armstrong, 1990) would suggest a more widespread use of diagnosis and testing for fitness. However, the limitations and inadequacies of the presently and easily controlled tests have been voiced by Armstrong (1987) and Fox and Biddle (1987). If these limitations can be overcome, perhaps through modern technology, then a more widespread use of fitness testing could be forecast. However, the need for quick and easy usage and low cost is essential if they are to be used widely in schools. Perhaps more community-based and resource schemes would be the answer to the fitness needs of the community.

Motivation of Pupils

Motivation of pupils is the most pervasive and ubiquitous purpose, and we have already mentioned it under other headings. It can be the purpose behind the purpose so to speak, or at least a purpose which goes hand in hand with others. Thus certification, selection, feedback, selection of school teams are also motivational and are used as a motivational force by teachers. Even the way accountability works in the form of GCSE National Curriculum testing, ROA and reporting to parents are all motivating to the teacher in some way and used by them to motivate pupils. The teacher is constantly working at motivating the pupil as it is the intervening factor between pupil abilities and pupil attainments (Carroll, 1976a).

It must not be forgotten that assessment is a double-edged sword as far as motivation is concerned. If assessment is not positive, such as failure to get a qualification, gaining a low grade, negative feedback, diagnosis showing many weaknesses, failure to get into teams, it can be a demotivating force. So the assessment can quite easily fulfil the other purposes but fail to motivate.

In PE the activities and sports themselves are often thought to be their own motivation. For many people this is so, though clearly, this is not the same for everyone. Furthermore, the development of abilities and performance in most activities is enhanced by and thrives on competition, the results and evaluation of which are used to compare and judge performances against others (norm reference) and standards (criterion) and to motivate to further success and learning. Sport competitions are particularly used in this way. However, competition can emphasize pupils' lack of abilities or success, particularly when comparisons are made with others. Assessment and qualifications may also provide an additional source of motivation for those who are enthusiastic about PE activities, and may be the incentive needed for some pupils to achieve their best performances and fulfil their potential and increase their knowledge. However, it must also be remembered that motivation is an individual affair and that it must be related to the individual not to the activity as a whole. The SSEC (1963) forgot this when putting forward an argument against examinations,

> They are enjoyed for their own sake and for the pleasure of participation; they are their own motivation.

So too did the Schools Council (1977) when it added the following,

> The Council therefore considers an examination unnecessary and undesirable as a stimulus to interest and effort in physical education. (p. 15)

This also fails to acknowledge those pupils who are interested in the subject and wish to take the study of the subject further. Why should examinations not be used in such a way to stimulate interest and effort and to reach for higher standards? This purpose has been unashamedly used in governing body award schemes for many years by many PE teachers. The Government, too, is using test and examination results as a motivating force in an effort to raise standards of both teachers and pupils.

Selection

The most obvious examples of this purpose are selection for school teams and selection for employment or further/higher education based on examination results. It is also used within PE curriculum time itself for internal groupings for teaching purposes. There are clearly times when it is preferable to have homogeneous groupings of ability/performance for teaching or playing/performing in the interests of all standards of pupils. Informal assessment is usually carried out to make the groupings.

As already indicated under certification, PE has become part of the central selective mechanism for employment and further education when it entered GCSE and 'A' levels. Francis (1990) gives the example of an 'A' level PE student being accepted at the University of Oxford on the basis of the results of this 'A' level and two others.

Selection for school teams is the only purpose peculiar solely to PE. I have already indicated the importance to the PE teacher of school teams. There have been many claims for their virtues, for example, standards and excellence, pupils reaching their potential, social objectives and leisure opportunities (Glew, 1983). However, some of the claims would not stand up to close scrutiny, and they often involved a small proportion of the school population. Small primary schools did give opportunities for larger percentages of children to take part, but the larger secondary schools could not provide the same opportunities and many children who had represented the school at primary level were disappointed. School fixtures and competitions came under attack in the 1980s (Glew, 1983; Pollard, 1988) and their importance declined. However, as indicated earlier, the prevailing market economy approach to schooling means that extra-curricular activities including school fixtures may play an important role in the public image of the school. In the past selection has caused problems because the emphasis was often on winning rather than participation, selecting the 'best' team rather on widening the participation rate. This emphasis changed to some extent in the 1980s with the attack on competition. However, many people would agree with Rowntree (1977) that competition and selection are part of everyday life and pupils must be prepared for it. After all, they will meet them in work and leisure.

As indicated at the end of chapter 1, it is essential for teachers to be clear of their purposes in assessment. However, as can be seen from this chapter, these are likely to be varied and used in conjunction with each other. Assessments will be used for both formative and summative purposes, and this can cause confusion and conflict when they are asked to do too much, as in the case of the conflation of educational and political policies. Nevertheless, if teachers are clear why they are doing assessment this should help them to decide what and how to assess.

Chapter 3

What Can Teachers Assess in Physical Education?

Why is 'What' an Issue?

Teachers know what to assess, surely this is not an issue? However 'what can teachers assess in PE?' is not as simple a question as it seems. Life in classrooms, sports halls and playing fields is complex. Generally PE teachers do know what to assess for teaching purposes, but most of the objectives of PE raise issues in practical terms when it comes to their achievement and pupils' assessment. Extrapolating different skills, personal qualities and the varying elements and contributions within a performance and from each other, and providing evidence for them, is not an easy matter.

Before the advent of examinations, ROA and the National Curriculum when assessment was not an issue in PE, life was much simpler. It appeared that many teachers taught and then decided what to assess (Carroll, 1976a). In this model of teaching — assessment, the teacher decides to teach an activity, say volleyball, and will teach the skills needed for the game, such as the serve and dig, and then assess the pupils' techniques, their skills in applying them and overall performance. This worked well enough for feedback purposes and in the teaching situation. However these performances also included effort, attitude and personal characteristics as an integral part of the performance. These could be assessed generally for school team selection or reports and used or ignored as the teacher thought fit. Reports usually required an overall grade for attainment and another for effort and these were normally on a five-point norm reference system (Carroll, 1976b and 1980). Carroll (1976a) points out the importance of pupils' effort in the teachers' scheme of teaching, assessment and evaluation.

In the era of examinations, ROA and the National Curriculum the approaches of teach first then decide what to assess, of norm referencing and the dominance of effort are inadequate. For the new developments the teaching-assessment model demands an objectives type, criterion-reference model. Here the objectives and the criteria for assessment must be precise and clearly identified, and related to each other. PE assessments had often been characterized by their vagueness and generality, so it is not surprising that many teachers found difficulty in being precise enough when it came to making CSE Mode 3 submissions or including assessment practices in PE syllabuses. A problem for PE teachers, which many of their colleagues in other subjects avoid by concentrating solely on cognitive skills, is that many of the objectives are not easily assessable, some are long term,

Table 7: Summary of assessment objectives in GCSE, National Curriculum and ROA

GCSE	Show what pupil knows, understands, can do.		
Summary of all examining groups' syllabuses	Perform in 4/5 activities (skills, techniques etc.) Practical	Knowledge and understanding of Physical basis (sports science, HRF etc.) Activities (rules, tactics Social Issues (sport in society etc.) Written	Analysis and evaluation of performance Research skills (NEAB) Written
National Curriculum	Knowledge, skills, and processes pupils are expected to attain		
Summary of 4 ES	Perform in 6 activities (KS1,2) 4 activities (KS3) 2 activities (KS4) Different roles Planning and composing Practical	Knowledge and understanding of Exercise and healthy lifestyles Activities Different roles Community resources Oral, written, practical	Analysis and Evaluation of performance oral, written
ROA	Record pupils' achievement in Performance Examinations National Curriculum	Extra Curricular Personal qualities Cross curricular	Self evaluation Teacher evaluation

and some deal with personal and social qualities. Many PE teachers too, claim they are just as interested in the process as well as the product. Therefore what PE teachers have to do is to come to terms with the requirements of the modern developments in relation to the new teaching-assessment model.

Examinations concentrate on cognitive and psychomotor skills, whilst ROA involves recording these skills and also personal qualities (DES, 1989a). The National Curriculum, whilst emphasizing practical performance, also demands assessment of the processes of planning and evaluating performance which have rarely been formally assessed in the past, and a knowledge component invariably included only in examination syllabuses. What is particularly notable about all these developments is the explicit formulation of a criterion-reference system.

The objectives which are required to be assessed or recorded in GCSE, ROA, and the National Curriculum have been summarized in table 7. In the GCSE the objectives to be assessed are very clearly identified in each of the syllabuses, and it is also clear that all of them cover the same basic ground and processes. Carroll (1990a and 1991) identified three components within these objectives as performance, knowledge and understanding, and analysis and evaluation, and showed that the first two dominated the assessment. These three components can also be identified in the National Curriculum through its End of Key Stage Statements. Performance is not surprisingly the main component, but knowledge and understanding and evaluation gain a prominence in the 5–16 curriculum, which had been lacking before. ROA is different from the other two developments in type but is used to record the pupils' performance, skills and knowledge and allows the opportunity for self-appraisal and evaluation. A more precise formulation of assessment objectives related to weightings and methods of assessment is given in table 8 through an example from the NEA GCSE PE syllabus. The more detailed criteria for practical performance and the personal study are shown in the syllabus, whilst the criteria for the written examination

Table 8: Showing NEAB GCSE objectives and weightings related to methods

The candidate will be able to:
  (i) demonstrate competence in the chosen physical activities as specified in the subject content;
 (ii) display, as appropriate, a knowledge and understanding of laws, rules, techniques, strategies and safety factors relating to the chosen sports or physical activities;
(iii) display a knowledge and understanding of the physical basis of performance and exercise in physical activities;
 (iv) display a knowledge of the organization of sports and physical activities in this country and of the social influences in participation;
  (v) demonstrate the skills of research, analysis and evaluation within a selected area of physical education.

Objective	% Weighting	Methods and Weightings		
		Practical	Written Paper	Personal Study
1,2	50	50		
3,4	30		30	
5	20			20
Totals	100	50	30	20

papers are seen through the mark scheme and examiners' reports available after the examination. The GCSE schemes show good examples of the planning of, and relation between, objectives, content and assessment, which had been lacking in most PE syllabuses (see Underwood, 1983).

I am going to examine the 'what can teachers assess?' question by using an objectives model. It is difficult to divorce the 'what' from the 'how' question (the way that it is done) in raising issues, and inevitably the method of assessment will be touched upon, but detailed examination of the 'how' will appear in the next chapter.

The Objectives Model

By using this model it is meant that the skills, knowledge, abilities and qualities the teacher wants the pupil to possess or improve upon in a course are identified beforehand. Each objective should be identified in terms of pupil outcomes, as in the GCSE case in table 8. There may be other pupil effects which may not be stated, and which may or may not be assessable, and teachers might be unaware that they are assessing other qualities (see chapter 9; and Rowntree, 1977). If the PE literature and official documents, such as Kane (1974) Hendry (1978) Underwood (1983) and DES documents are examined, the objectives of PE can be categorized as follows;

- physical skills/competence in activities;
- leisure and lifestyles;
- personal and social qualities and skills/development;
- physical development, health and fitness;
- cognitive skills/development;
- aesthetic awareness and understanding.

Let us take a look at what can be assessed in these categories.

Physical Skills and Competence in Activities

Can Teachers Assess Pupils' Physical Skills and Competence?

This is the area where there is least controversy and argument as to what can be assessed. The central product in PE is in this area because the main focus in teaching is physical activities, which are often used as vehicles for more than physical objectives, such as social development. In GCSE and the National Curriculum prominence is given to practical performance requirements. For some activities the assessment is often a purely objective exercise, for example in athletics and swimming where objective measures of time or distance assess performance. Here the end result is the assessment. It is of course a reliable and valid measure and is used in the Governing Bodies of Sport Award Schemes and in the GCSE. It is also supplemented by the assessment of technique in the GCSE. It is interesting to note that 'to swim 25 yards' is an End of Key Stage 2 Statement and the only statement with a specific objective requirement in the National Curriculum (DES, 1992). This is an excellent example of criterion referencing because it states a specific standard. In the GCSE and award schemes the criteria for marks is stated in terms of times and distances, but the tables for these were based on the idea of norm differentiation so were norm reference in basic design.

The advantage of this objective assessment in athletics and swimming is that it can be looked at without reference to the performance of other pupils. It can be purely ipsative and used to assess progress or lack of it. Many other physical activities can be looked at in relation to an objective score, for example, in games the number of points or goals scored may be seen as a measure of the effectiveness of overall play. However, these assessments cannot be seen without reference to the performances of other people, namely the opposition, and in team games other members of the team. This is where part of the difficulty lies. Individual performances do depend on other peoples' performances also.

How well individual skills are performed can be assessed by observing the way they are performed and the effectiveness of that particular part of the performance. When it is broken down in this way it can be reduced to a technical exercise, an analysis of techniques, for example, positions of shoulders, swing of the racket, foot work in a badminton skill. To do this of course the PE teacher must have that detailed knowledge of the technique. However there is more to playing badminton and any other game than a series of techniques and skills, there is the decision making processes of shot selection, anticipation, and tactical awareness. The essence of many activities is the contest, the competition with an opponent, therefore the analysis of the decision-making processes, and the carrying out of tactics and different styles of play can only be done in relation to an opposition. Team games provide more complex situations where team colleagues and their positional and styles of play are also considered. However, the carrying out of techniques and application of skill also includes to a greater or a lesser extent physical qualities such as reaction time, speed, power, strength, stamina, and personal qualities such as motivation, determination and attitude to competition, which are all an integral part of performance (see figure 5). It is possible to identify which pupils possess these qualities by an observant teacher, but it is impossible to separate them from the performance and to say how much is contributed by the different qualities. Different activities require different qualities in different proportions and pupils possess and utilize these qualities in different proportions according to the situation and response to the situation. The difficulty for knowledgeable staff is not in applying the criteria and judging the level of performance. The difficulty in normal PE lessons and the National Curriculum is in coping with large numbers of pupils and seeing them in relatively small amounts of time in varying contexts. There is not always enough time to provide and observe *all* pupils in a varied number of contexts to show what they can achieve. This appears to be getting more difficult too with the squeeze on PE time. In the context of GCSE, there is initial difficulty in giving a mark or grade. This difficulty is soon overcome with studying the criteria and going to a standardization or moderating session.

In games, an analysis of performance could be reduced to a quantitative game analysis to include which skills are selected and when, reading of opponent's game and responding accordingly, applying tactics in offence or counteract in defence. However a simple analysis is unlikely to give the complete picture of a player, and an accurate recorded game analysis on any sort of regular basis would be time consuming and out of the question, though there is no reason why pupils could not be taught how to do it for GCSE, 'A' level PE and Key Stage 4 of the National Curriculum to deal with the evaluation component. Game analysis is a good diagnostic tool which would be useful for teaching, showing strengths and weaknesses not easily identified, and judging the performances of others as well as gaining knowledge of their own game. Because of the impracticality of recorded game analysis, PE teachers have to observe these dimensions of a pupil's game/performance and gain a general impression so it does require a perceptive teacher and one who can weigh up these dimensions quickly. Experienced PE teachers are generally used to this and are good at it, but now they need to be explicit in their criteria and need to apply this to all pupils in their charge. What is clearly apparent is that a whole performance assessment is inclusive of a range of skills and qualities, physical, cognitive and affective. With individual activities where competition is not directly against other individuals such as in gymnastics, trampolining, canoeing, and climbing, assessment can be based on technical competence — qualitative judgment as to how well the performance compares to the ideal technique. Dance and possibly educational gymnastics may be given an assessment for technical merit but, in addition, there are more artistic, expressive and aesthetic elements. For dance too there may be other criteria used such as choreography. In these activities unlike games, the pupil's performance is influenced less by the performance of others.

The acquisition of skill is not a unitary dimension, nor is it a case of 'can do it' or 'cannot do it'. There are different levels in the acquisition and application of skill related to quality (technical efficiency, level of refinement, effectiveness of outcome), quantity (frequency of production), complexity of context, and application of skill. The teacher has to identify these levels. This can be likened to identifying cognitive processes as in Bloom's Taxonomy of cognitive skills, and Peel's classification (see under cognitive objectives in this chapter, table 10 and chapter 5). Walters (1991) has in fact used Peel's theory to identify processes in GCSE practical work. However, this model is cognitive and does not include all the elements needed to identify the levels of practical performance.

Harrow (1972) suggests a framework for a taxonomy of the psychomotor domain consisting of:

1 Reflex movements.
2 Basic-Fundamental movements.
3 Perceptual abilities (kinesthetic etc.).
4 Physical abilities (strength etc.).
5 Skilled movements.
6 Non-Discursive communication (expressive etc.).

PE teachers will not be concerned with the first two stages unless they are involved with remedial work. Perceptual abilities are fundamental to physical performance and such aspects as developing body awareness, kinesthetic senses, visual and auditory stimuli, and hand-eye coordination are strong in the early years of schooling. Physical abilities in this context mean components which are usually classified under physical development or fitness, and are of course of concern throughout the whole school programme. Non-discursive communication includes expression and aesthetic as a particular objective in dance throughout the school. The skilled movement category is the one we are most concerned with here. Harrow (*ibid*) identifies three sub-domains, simple, compound, complex adaptive skills and each one divided into beginners, intermediate, advanced and highly skilled. Compound adaptive skills include basic skills plus the management of implements, as in the case of racket sports. The complex adaptive category requires the greater mastery of body mechanics as in difficult gymnastic movements. The PE teacher is required to assess the degree of proficiency of these skills, and the dimensions for this need to be identified.

A model by Cameron (1991), which was adapted from a model of learning by White and Harvey (1980), has been used as a framework for curriculum-related assessment. This model provides a useful basis for adaptation and then to view the levels of acquisition of skills. My adapted model is shown in table 9. This model suggests dimensions to judge the level of performance, the level of refinement, frequency of production, fluency and speed in production, and application to different contexts. These dimensions should not be seen as a hierarchy, because basic unrefined skills may be produced frequently or at speed and applied to different situations, before skills have been refined. These dimensions will however help the teacher to determine the level of competence and performance.

Leisure and Active Lifestyles

Can Teachers Assess Pupils' Leisure Activities and Active Lifestyles?

Education for leisure has been an important objective in PE for many years now (see Kane, 1974; Hendry, 1978; Underwood, 1983; DES, 1991b) and has received impetus from official reports, for example, the Wolfenden Report (1960), the Newsom Report (1963) and the School Sport Forum (1988). The aim has been to teach the pupils activities after which they could participate in them in their own

Table 9: Model of skill acquisition showing dimensions for assessing level [1]

Acquisition of Skill (Quality)	— Basic — can do it, low level of technique
	— Refined — Good technique
	Error reduction
	Effectiveness of outcome
Maintenance / Frequency (Quantity)	— Can reproduce
	Skill retention
	Consistency
Fluency / Speed (Quality, Context)	— Can do at speed
	Can do under pressure
Application of Skills (Context)	— To different, new situations
	Reproduce variations
	Increasing complexity
	— Understands Principles Answers Problems

1 Adapted from Cameron (1991).

time and particularly when they had left school. This idea has much in common with the more recent 'active lifestyles' philosophy brought on by a concern for health (see Armstrong, 1990), and in this respect is linked to the health and fitness issue. The 'leisure' objective was usually attempted through an options programme in the fourth and fifth years. However in the past, in many schools the direct link with people, clubs and facilities in the local community was often minimal or non-existent. Moreover, this 'leisure' objective did not become a central focus within the school, so there was rarely support from elsewhere in the school. More recently joint school-community schemes have made these direct links, for example, in Coventry and in Birmingham (see BBC *Panorama*, 1987; Murdoch, 1990; Laventure, 1992), and these have had more success than previously.

ROA demand a recognition of not only extra-curricular school activities but also of out-of-school interests which do indicate leisure interests and lifestyles. The National Curriculum rationale includes '. . . and teaches pupils to value the benefits of participation in physical activity while in school and throughout life'. Presumably this means more than to know the value of physical activity, and implies to value it is to follow its principles and lead an active lifestyle. This is followed up in the Attainment Target.

> . . . and decide where to focus their involvement in physical activity for a healthy and enjoyable lifestyle. (KS3, DES, 1992)

and again,

> prepare and carry out and monitor personal programmes for a healthy and enjoyable lifestyle, considering the use of community resources where appropriate. (KS4, DES, 1992)

Some of the GCSE syllabuses include knowledge of local provision, for example NEA, and SEG, but of course, this is not the same thing as participation or leading an active lifestyle. One of the problems for the PE teacher is the assessment of this objective. In the past the teacher could just hope that the children would take up some activity or another — it was more of a long term aim. The GCSE has shown it is possible to test the knowledge aspect of local provision by traditional methods, but ROA and the National Curriculum go further, and these can only be assessed by the children telling what they do in their own time.This immediately raises two important issues which can easily be overlooked in the excitement of pushing for what one believes in:

(i) personal freedom — social control; should pupils have the right to choose their own lifestyles and reject others? Is this a form of surveillance? (see Hargreaves, 1989, chapter 7);

(ii) equality of opportunity, all children do not have the same opportunities, access, family support and role models.

In spite of the excellent section in the National Curriculum proposals (DES, 1991b) on the issues related to equal opportunity in respect of special educational needs, gender and cultural diversity, social disadvantage is neglected. Sparkes (1991b) warns of the dangers of following an individualistic approach and ignoring social structures and immediate social frameworks in which decisions are taken. It is clear that all pupils do not have the same opportunities and certain pupils are going to be disadvantaged. Leaving these issues aside, the problem now is that leisure interests, knowledge of, and participation in active lifestyles must be commented upon. It can be done through pupils' own recording or the diary method, and room found for these in formative documents for ROA. Knowledge about local provision and planning programmes can be done through traditional methods of assessing knowledge — oral, written and project, as has been done in GCSE. However, it is one thing to record the interest involvement and participation on a frequency and perhaps time level, it is another to determine the quality, or the activity level of that lifestyle. Clearly pupil involvement in this assessment is the only practical way to deal with it.

Personal and Social Competences and Qualities

What Personal and Social Competences of the Pupils Can Teachers Assess?

I have lumped these skills and qualities together because it is very difficult to separate many of them when it comes to practice. Personal qualities do not exist in a vacuum. They are utilized in a social context. Personal and social competences have always been seen to be very important in PE (see Kane, 1974; Carroll, 1980). Hendry (1975 and 1978) in fact emphasizes the priority of social competences in PE in England based on empirical evidence, but shows a lower priority in Scotland. However Carroll (1980) points out the lack of clarity, and the multiplicity of meanings in the use of concepts such as 'social'. He also shows the lack of assessment on these dimensions, and shows the way they are hidden in behavioural and effort comments and gradings. Carroll (*ibid*) also agreed with Ward and Hardman's (1978) findings that PE teachers were concerned with particularistic anticipated pupil effects rather than broad general objectives which were not clearly well defined enough to be able to utilize and assess in the teaching situation. What teachers found useful was to assess effort and behaviour for teaching and reports (Carroll, 1976a, 1976b and 1980). The importance of these dimensions were clearly identified in teachers' perception of pupils and were used as a basis for educational identity, for example, in the troublemaker, skiver, athlete and enthusiast (Carroll, 1986b). In these empirical studies, Carroll clearly identifies the teachers' criteria for these 'types' of pupils and the effort dimension. Behaviour and effort do not appear to be a problem for the teacher.

According to the government, personal qualities should be included in ROA and 'reliability' and 'enthusiasm' are given as examples for inclusion (DES, 1989a). An examination of a number of ROA in use including published versions, such as, Booton (1986), Hatfield and Phillips (1989), reveal the following recorded qualities, independence, initiative, honesty, reliability, determination, self-esteem, self-confidence: self-realization, emotional stability, cooperation with others, and leadership. There is a real problem here for teachers to decide which personal qualities to include and the ones which can be assessed satisfactorily.

Examinations and National Curriculum ES do not demand an assessment of personal qualities *per se*, though the rationale for the National Curriculum does include self esteem and confidence and coping with success and failure:

> helps to establish self esteem through the development of physical con-
> fidence and helps pupils to cope with the success and failure in competitive
> and cooperative activities. (DES, 1991b, p. 5)

and again,

> In order to develop positive attitudes pupils should be encouraged to:
>
> > observe the conventions of fair play, honest competition and
> > good sporting behaviour;
> >
> > understand and cope with a variety of outcomes, including both
> > success and failure;
> >
> > be aware of the effects and consequences of their actions on
> > others and on the environment. (DES, 1992, p. 3)

It is, of course, easy to provide the situations which offer opportunities to achieve the above aims and the programmes of study do that (see DES, 1991b, Paras 8.51 and 8.70) but it is not always easy to assess these aims. Some of these personal and social objectives are much easier to assess than others.

The problem is what counts as evidence? Evidence is usually intangible and variable, and is conflated with other qualities and with the performance. The teacher has to deal with these qualities as attitudes at the behavioural level. However actions may be interpreted in different ways. For example, what is cooperation with others? — Is it compliance to teachers' and other pupils' demands? If a pupil argues with the teacher or other pupils, is this evidence of lack of cooperation, standing up for oneself, not accepting authority or independence? Children have been known to be punished for speaking their minds, which in other contexts may be regarded as 'honest', 'independent thinkers'. Leadership is thought to be a good quality, but compliant followers are needed to show this quality, other-wise there would be conflicts and non cooperation. Where is the dividing line between a leader and someone who likes to be bossy, which is not usually thought to be a good trait. There are fine lines too, between using initiative and independence and being stupid and not asking for advice in more challenging and dangerous pursuits. Is someone who will not take part in extra-curricular activities or will not play for the school team not enthusiastic or not loyal to the school? And a pupil who devotes himself to the pursuit of excellence in sport and is single minded (good traits) is likely also to be 'selfish' and 'uncooperative' in most sporting contexts. For example, such a pupil may not play with lower ability pupils, and their participation may be at the expense of others by monopolizing facilities.

Any individual's performance will include many personal qualities which are not easy to extrapolate from the context, and they may be context-related so statements themselves should be context-related. The National Curriculum will make demands on personal qualities in different contexts such as in 'responding to challenging tasks' and 'sustain energetic activity' at the end of KS2. Although many people do act consistently across different contexts, there is no evidence to suggest that these qualities are context free. Therefore it is important that comments about personal qualities are set in context. It is often easier for primary teachers to get to know all their pupils well because they see them in so many situations and for considerably longer periods of time than secondary PE specialists who have to see large numbers of pupils for shorter periods of time. Personal and social qualities may be best dealt with in PSE as cross-curricular qualities, but if so, the point about context must be borne in mind. Another important point is that the evidence in many instances is open to different interpretations as indicated above. Sometimes the judgment can say more about the teacher than the pupil. It is equally important for the pupil to get to know him/herself, his/her own qualities and limitations, and be involved in self-appraisal in different contexts.

Physical Development, Health and Fitness

Should Teachers Test Pupils' Physical Fitness?

There has been a tremendous growth in the interest in what has become known as 'health-related fitness' or 'health-related activity' as part of physical education, witness the HEA and PEA Health and PE project which has now been running for several years (see HEA/PEA Newsletter), the Happy Heart Project for primary children (see Sleap, 1990). Consequently there has been a growth of interest in fitness testing. The extent to which fitness tests are used is not known, but a small survey of twenty-nine schools in a selected region showed that approximately 90 per cent of both boys and girls departments used fitness tests in some way (Snailham, 1990). The types of tests used were dominated by the use of AAHPERD Fitness Test Battery, for example standing long jump, sit ups, twelve minute run/walk, vertical jump (*ibid*). On the surface, fitness testing would seem to be a most desirable form of assessment and one that is objective, useful and motivational. However the use of fitness tests in schools is more complex and fraught with difficulties (Armstrong, 1987 and 1990; Fox and Biddle, 1986). These tests measure different aspects of fitness, for example, strength of particular muscle groups (for example, press ups), speed (for example, shuttle run), power (for example, jumps), stamina (for example, runs) cardio-respiratory fitness (for example, VO2 max, the rate oxygen can be consumed through running on a treadmill), flexibility (for example, sit and reach), and bodily composition (for example, skin fold test on selected parts of the body). Their use has been prompted by hitec instruments and modern technology at affordable prices.

Armstrong (1987 and 1990) and Fox and Biddle (1987) have criticized fitness tests on the grounds that they are affected by the child's growth factor, motivation, skill level, test conditions and by uncontrollable fundamental components such as genetic and motivational level. They show that genetics may account for possibly 50–60 per cent of the score whilst training may account for a further 20–40 per cent depending on the test (*ibid*). This in fact may be no different from many cognitive tests in schools. I know of no tests which to a certain extent are not motivational, skill-related, utilize genetic factors or susceptible to test conditions. Verbal reasoning tests for example will be effected by genetics and motivational levels. It is perhaps not the tests themselves which should be of most concern, although Armstrong (1990) does warn that some tests are not 'based on sound physiological principles' (but he does not say which). It is possibly the knowledge of the teachers about the test limitations and the use of the results in schools which should be more worrying. The part played by genetics and motivation must be acknowledged, and it would be difficult to show that any improvement in test scores are due to these factors or the exercise. However, there is a percentage which can be improved through exercise, and there is no reason why this cannot be attempted and tested if used in the right way. Certainly norms based on chronological age which fail to take into consideration maturational levels (skeletal and muscular development) will not be of much use for comparison and will be misleading (*ibid*). Fitness tests may be a motivational source, though they may also have the opposite effect with some children particularly if handled badly or the results used unwisely, such as in the incorrect use of norm tables and norm referencing. However, individual use for diagnostic purposes or self referencing to see progress may be appropriate. Fox and Biddle (1988) found that research shows that it is the process of regular exercise which modifies blood fat levels and controls body fat and Armstrong (1990) relates exercise levels to coronary heart disease. Therefore it is better to concentrate on the exercise level aspect rather than the test results.

What is perhaps important is that children know the limitations themselves, how testing can be carried out and used suitably, and how they can personally monitor their own fitness and exercise programmes. What I am suggesting is an educational use of fitness testing which has become part of GCSE syllabuses and health related activity programmes.

All the GCSE syllabuses include the knowledge of and use of fitness tests but the pupils fitness *per se* is not assessable. The Hong Kong equivalent of the British GCSE gives 15 per cent to the pupils' fitness, and this seems an inappropriate use of fitness tests. The 'A' level PE syllabus too does include a section in the practical element which is meant to be a general physical preparation section but is basically a fitness type test, measuring flexibility, strength and speed. It does not appear to serve the purpose for which it was intended and also appears to suffer from gender inequalities. This also seems an inappropriate use of fitness tests in 'A' level. It would not be a surprise to see this removed from the syllabus after a SEAC review.

In the earlier stages of the National Curriculum the emphasis is on promoting cardiovascular efficiency, strength, endurance and flexibility but KS4 includes,

> They should be guided to understand design, plan for, monitor and record appropriately programmes to improve fitness. (DES, 1991b)

and again as an example at the ES. KS4,

> be taught to understand how to organise and monitor an activity schedule that leads to an improvement in fitness. (DES, 1992)

This would point to the need to understand fitness testing, which is, as indicated, already present in the GCSE. There is clearly room here for links with science and health education and technology in cross-curricular themes and skills. For example in technology. Skinsley's use of the JCR and Scottish Health Education Councils 'Fit to Eat' tests (includes a section on HRF test) are examples which have been used (Skinsley, 1987; Snailham, 1990). This type of work with discussion of the limitations and ipsative referencing are more appropriate.

It is clear that physical fitness can be measured but there are queries over the validity and reliability of the tests for use in schools and the meaning and use of results. Just as pupils' National Curriculum levels compounded into league tables and norms are an inappropriate use of these results, though they are being so used, so the testing of pupils' fitness related to norms is inappropriate. Hopefully the Government will not try this one on when the next scare about physical activity levels in children comes along (see BBC *Panorama* (1987) and ITV *Dispatches* (1992) programmes for this scare, and the link to the armed forces fitness tests).

Cognitive

Which Pupils' Cognitive Skills Can Be Assessed in PE?

Only a few years ago, the question would be regarded as hardly worth asking. Traditionally, PE was regarded as practical and there was no academic or theoretical work (see Carroll, 1982). The advent of CSE changed that. It is not that PE teachers were not aware of its cognitive content — all practical work involves thought processes and decision making as an important dimension in open skills games. But here the cognitive is an inherent part of the physical performance and any informal assessment of these processes, for example, the use of tactics, is within the whole practical performance. There is no dual body-mind dichotomy here. The advent of CSE changed the curriculum for the fourth and fifth years. Most of the CSE examination boards demanded theoretical work — it was no doubt a status question and what counts as worthwhile knowledge (*ibid*). However, it was not only that. Many PE teachers did believe that there was a large body of knowledge forming the basis of physical performance (anatomy and physiology), knowledge related to specific activities (for example, rules, tactics), knowledge related to taking part in physical activities and sport (for example, where to participate in local facilities, social issues). These knowledge components

Table 10: Cognitive processes identified by Bloom (1956) and Peel (1971)

Bloom (1956)	Peel (1971)
Knowledge Recall	Describer
Comprehension	Explainer -Understanding
Application	What is required
Analysis	Cause and effect
Synthesis	Specific-General Link
Evaluation	

have been included in GCSE syllabuses which have to show what children know, understand and can do. The first component mentioned above, the basis of physical performance, is inherent and fundamental to health-related activity and fitness programmes, and all three components have become part of the National Curriculum at some stage.

What is particularly interesting is that though much of the knowledge can be taught in the practical setting or through what can be termed in a 'practical way' by collecting information, it was often taught in a traditional manner such as talk and chalk (*ibid*) and it was assessed in both the CSE and GCSE through traditional techniques, for example written work. The 'A' level Sports Studies has chosen to assess the whole of its syllabus in this way, and the 'A' level PE syllabus is mainly theoretical and assessed mainly through written work. Both of the 'A' levels have strong academic disciplines as their basis.

So what is it that is being assessed under the 'theoretical' and cognitive banners? What processes are being included? In GCSE knowledge and understanding is strong in all the components mentioned above (see tables 7 and 8). However as Bloom (1956) and Peel (1971) amongst others have shown, understanding is not a single concept or process. Whereas knowledge may be regarded as the descriptive level and assessed via recall, understanding can be regarded as a multi-level hierarchical concept (see table 10). Walters (1991) using Peelian theory (Peel, 1971) shows the different types of understanding, for example, understanding what is required, understanding cause and effect, linking of specific elements to more general concepts ('Games for understanding'), and the hierarchical nature from simple accounts (describer) to a more abstract understanding (explainer) are reflected in practical performance. He shows that levels of understanding have been related to criteria for the marking of practical work in a GCSE syllabus. Clearly this type of analysis can be applied to non-examination PE as well. Rowntree (1977) discusses Bloom's cognitive taxonomy (Bloom, 1956) which includes the following processes: knowledge, comprehension, application, analysis, synthesis and evaluation (see table 10). The first three of these are clearly portrayed in both practical and theoretical GCSE assessment. As Carroll (1991) has shown in GCSE syllabuses, analysis and practical evaluation are much more limited in their appearance, and examples are sometimes hard to find. The best examples are to be found in the NEA project, and the WJEC video presentation-analysis. This type of analysis can also be applied to non-examination PE.

The interim proposals for the National Curriculum suggested three Attainment Targets (1) planning and composing; (2) performing; and (3) appraisal and evaluation (DES, 1991a). In the final report, under pressure from the Minister, these were merged into one Attainment Target. The rationale for this change is the integral and holistic value of the three strands in effective performance. These have been reflected in statutory End of Key Stage statements and non-statutory levels of attainment (DES, 1991b and 1992). An emphasis on planning and composing certainly brings in cognitive and creative skills. The National Curriculum lays greater emphasis on these processes than has traditionally been done in many schools, though it has existed and been carried out through such activities as devising games in junior schools, composing gymnastic sequences and dance movements, planning and trying out different tactical moves and plans in games, planning an expedition in outdoor pursuits, planning training routines in athletics. The evaluative processes are necessary to judge how well the performance is carried out against a criteria in technical skills and against performance of others and self. However, what has really changed is the emphasis placed on the pupil doing all of these things and being assessed in these processes. In the past, in most activities except possibly in educational gymnastics and dance, most of the planning and certainly most of the evaluating was done by the teacher. It was the teacher who said whether performances were 'good' or bad', although, not always why. The National Curriculum appears to put greater emphasis on pupils' understanding and from a much earlier age, for example, at Key Stage 1,

Describe what they and others are doing.

Recognise the effects of physical activity on their bodies. (DES, 1992)

and again in ES Key Stage 2.

be able to sustain energetic activity over periods of time and understand the effects on the body. (DES, 1992, p. 6)

These objectives are getting at understanding cause and effect relationships. Clearly it will be best done in the practical situation, however, as the teacher is not assessing the effects on the body, but the knowledge and understanding of the effects, the assessment must be through oral or written mode. Similarly, children are now asked to evaluate their own and others' performances.

evaluate how well they and others perform against criteria suggested by the teacher, and suggest ways of improving performance. (ES, KS2) (DES, 1992)

understand and evaluate how well they and others have achieved what they set out to do, appreciate strengths and weaknesses and suggest ways of improving. (ES, KS3) (DES, 1992, p. 8)

These objectives involve an advanced form of understanding. They require the ability to analyze, not only at the concrete level, technical, tactical and compositional skills especially, but also the application of principles at an abstract level. Asking the pupils to show how they can improve these skills is similar to asking them how to solve a problem. It is interesting to note that in 'A' level PE syllabus, this type of understanding and evaluation is carried out within the practical performance component through an oral assessment but it is of course time consuming. This does mean that students who do not get high marks for practical performance can still score highly on analysis and evaluation within the practical performance section. The processes of observation, analysis and evaluation which are being assessed here, are required for 'intelligent' spectating and effective teaching and coaching. These encompass different roles to the traditional performer only role in PE.

It is clear from the above discussion that the cognitive domain is strong within PE, and that different aspects of the domain can be assessed both through practical and theoretical performances. The teacher must choose the appropriate mode for the child and the process.

Aesthetic Development

Can Teachers Assess Aesthetic Development and Qualities?

Aesthetic development as an objective has featured in surveys such as Kane (1974) and Underwood (1983), and is present in the NC rationale for PE (DES, 1991b). However, there seems to be some confusion in the use of the term 'aesthetics'. It is often used only in relation to the activities of dance and possibly gymnastics, or is often used synonymously with the concept of 'beauty' only. Perhaps this is not surprising when there is lack of agreement over the meaning of the concept among philosophers and experts (see Meakin, 1980; Kirk, 1984). The confusion is also maintained by the fact that there are two types of activities. There are those activities that have an end objective independent of the way the activity is performed, for example, in soccer the objective is to score goals, and there are those where the end product is not independent of the manner it is performed, for example, in gymnastics where the manner of the performance is the end objective and is usually regarded as 'aesthetic'. But this does not mean to say that activities such as soccer cannot be aesthetic or gymnastics cannot have technical or physical or functional purposes. However, one must get away from the view that aesthetics is an inherent quality of the activities and come to see that it is related to the responses and feelings of those performing or attending to the activity (Meakin, 1980; Kirk, 1984). Therefore to take an aesthetic stance is a particular way of responding or behaving, as opposed to other ways, such as moral or technical. So what does this 'aesthetic' include? According to Aspin (1974) and Kirk (1984), it involves an emotional response in relation to criteria and standards, and this response will be positive and relate to 'satisfaction'. The problem with this is that it does presuppose 'standards' and knowledge and is open to the criticism of individual relativism, as exemplified in the expression 'beauty is in the eye of the beholder'. Many people have an emotional response, which may be regarded as 'aesthetic', but they do not always know the reason why. What this means is that they are not aware of their 'criteria'. Wilson (1986) has likened them to being in love. Is it that, as in this state, people can respond aesthetically but have no real aesthetic understanding? Are the criteria and standards at a 'subconscious' level? Perhaps this is what aesthetic education is all about, — either bringing to the consciousness aesthetic criteria and standards, or making people aware of the aesthetic criteria and standards so they can make discriminating judgments. This is what appears to be demanded by Wilson (*ibid*) and Howard and Laws (1989) suggestion that the aesthetic must be focused upon specifically like many other objectives. At the present time it appears merely to be a hoped for by-product of performance in the PE curriculum, and judging by a survey by Howard and Laws (*ibid*), not very successful at that. They found that only four students out of 120 training to be PE teachers had encountered the concept 'aesthetic' in relation to PE, and 74 per cent saw no relevance between sport and aesthetics.

You will note that above, I used the concepts 'perform' and 'attend to' in relation to aesthetics. Best (1974) and Meakin (1980) have argued that the participant can have aesthetic responses as well as the spectator. This is an extremely important point for PE as it has implications for the PE curriculum and assessment. It may be taught and assessed through the roles of performer and spectator, and this is something the National Curriculum has taken up. It has been difficult enough to say what 'aesthetic' development is, so the assessment of the aesthetic promises to be more problematic. This is because it has been defined as an emotional response, a set of feelings against an aesthetic criteria. I expected the Assessment of Performance Unit (APU) aesthetic development report to be useful here but is only marginally so (AEB APU, 1983). The report distinguishes between artistic development (related to the arts) and aesthetic development, and in spite of its title, bases its model on artistic development. This does include aesthetic experience as the 'irreducible component'. Clearly assessing pupils' responses and feelings is not going to be easy. In the first instance the teacher has to find out what they are. Perhaps this can be done by working in pairs in the teaching-learning context, perhaps even recorded in formative ROA. But what if the feelings, the aesthetic responses, do not coincide with the teacher's? In this case, the teacher will have to accept the difference. And what about the other part of the equation, the aesthetic criteria to which the 'feelings' are related? This is more promising because there is something more tangible here, for example, the form, flow, rhythm (which is probably underpinned by technical merit), and in certain circumstances, such as in dance, expression and mood. If the pupils have an understanding of these types of things then they know what to respond to.

Part of the difficulty of assessment may be solved if aesthetic development can be assessed through performance, difficult though that may be. However does a gymnastic performance which can be described as aesthetic by the teacher in itself mean that the pupil has a well-developed sense of the aesthetic? And has a pupil who cannot perform the same gymnastic movements in an aesthetically pleasing manner no awareness of the aesthetic? No not necessarily, according to the definition. In the first example, it may not be 'performed' or 'attended to' with aesthetic criteria in mind, or responded to with the 'aesthetic stance'. However, perhaps it could be if the teacher presented it within an aesthetic context and stance such as the way dance is often presented to portray feelings and moods. In the case of the second example the pupil may be fully aware of the aesthetic criteria but cannot perform it physically. Clearly then there must be the means of evaluating performance according to the 'aesthetic' criteria. This is what the National Curriculum clearly set out to do by mentioning it specifically in the non-statutory levels,

Table 11: Summary of objectives of PE related to examples

Objectives	Criteria (examples)	Examples in GCSE, ROA, NC	
Physical Competence and Skills	Technical Efficiency Application of skill Effectiveness Objective measurement	GCSE —	Demonstrate competence in chosen activities (NEA)
		ROA —	Record practical achievements, curricular and extra-curricular
		NC —	Practice and improve their performance (KS1) Adapt and refine existing skills and develop new skills safely across all activities (KS3)
Physical Development Health & Fitness	Strength Speed Stamina Flexibility	GCSE —	Through participation in activities. Through knowledge and understanding of fitness.
		ROA —	Personal records-self evaluation.
		NC —	Prepare a fitness programme . . . plan a fitness programme for different individuals . . . (KS4 POS). Through participation in physical activities.
Cognitive	Recall knowledge Understanding Evaluation	GCSE —	Display a knowledge of . . . (NEA, SEG). Demonstrate the skills of research, analysis and evaluation within a selected area of PE (NEA).
		ROA —	Self evaluation. Recording knowledge.
		NC —	Be made aware of the historical, social and cultural issues associated with the activities undertaken (KS4 POS).
Leisure and Active Lifestyle	Knowledge of value of regular exercise. Knowledge of community resources. Regular participation in extra-curricular and out-of-school activities.	GCSE —	The enjoyment of taking part in physical activities and their encouragement of their continuance in adult life (SEG Aims).
		ROA —	Record participation in physical activities.
		NC —	Prepare, carry out and monitor personal programmes for a healthy and enjoyable lifestyle, considering the use of community resources (KS4).
Social and Personal Qualities	Co-operation Reliability Leadership Responsibility	GCSE —	The development of personal attitudes and social qualities through a varity of situations and challenges (SEG Aims).
		ROA —	Record personal and social qualities.
		NC —	Be encouraged to adopt good sporting behaviour and recognise and reject antisocial responses including unfair play (KS2 POS).
Aesthetics	Emotional response	GCSE —	Describe and analyse through observation the qualities (including aesthetic and creative elements) specified physical activities (SEG).
		ROA —	Personal recording.
		NC —	In response to a range of stimuli express feelings, moods (KS2 POS). Be helped to explore and present different responses to a variety of tasks and stimuli (KS2 POS).

make simple judgments of their own and others' performance using aesthetic and functional criteria. (Level 4f)

apply aesthetic and functional criteria to their own or others' performance, and suggest how the performance could be improved. (Level 5e) (DES, 1991b)

However in the statutory ES (DES, 1992) the 'aesthetic' criteria is not mentioned specifically and so it will be left up to the teacher to introduce the 'aesthetic' stance. I suspect that many will not do so and that in any case many teachers and pupils will need help relating the aesthetic criteria to many of the activities taught. Care will have to be taken that it is not reduced merely to technical efficiency and skill, although that may play a part in understanding the aesthetic. It is at this point I would like to come back to the definition of aesthetic. This encompassed positive feelings, for example, satisfaction, beauty, and both Aspin (1974) and Kirk (1984) suggest that ugliness, sadness etc. cannot be seen as aesthetic. However, Kirk seems to miss the point that if something is assessed and evaluated against a criteria in an aesthetic stance, and if it is deemed to be 'ugly' or 'sad', then, although this may be 'unaesthetic' or not pleasing, it is still based on the aesthetic criteria. It is just that the response and feelings are at the other end (displeasure, disatisfaction) of the dimension. This type of response is necessary as well as the positive if teachers are to increase the pupils' powers of discrimination and judgment, which is what the evaluation process is all about. It appears that Wilson (1986) makes a strong point when he states, 'we cannot get far in education in this area unless we can identify the particular compulsions our pupils are under' (p. 106). This would be a good starting point.

Conclusion

The discussion of 'What can be assessed' has raised many issues and revealed that the assessment of most of the objectives is not straightforward. The objectives and their criteria are summarized in table 11 and related to examples in GCSE, ROA, and the National Curriculum. How that assessment can be carried out is discussed in the next chapters.

Chapter 4

How Can Practical Performance be Assessed Satisfactorily?

Having looked at what can and should be assessed, the question remains, 'How can it be assessed satisfactorily?' This question has been partly answered in chapter 1 under the headings of 'making sense of the judgment', 'modes of assessment' and 'principles of assessment' in an effort to understand assessment. So this detail will not be repeated but the reader will be referred to chapter 1 at the appropriate place. In the teaching situation, the question is partially answered through the teacher having clear purposes in mind as this will lead to the selection of modes of assessment and particular tasks and techniques. So the teacher must decide first of all whether the purpose is formative or summative, whether it is for feedback to the pupil, diagnostic, or for certification and selection for example (see chapter 2). The teacher will select the appropriate modes and methods such as continuous, terminal, practical task, theoretical or examination.

The assessment of performance in athletics and swimming in terms of times and distances poses no problems for the teacher as it is objective and reliable. All teachers will measure the same performance in the same way and get the same result. Problems only occur when performances under different conditions are compared, for example, in athletics the type of track and weather conditions can make a substantial effect on times. Therefore, where these types of objective measurements are to be translated into marks, as in GCSE, then consideration must be given to the conditions under which the performance took place.

The assessment of physical performances in open contexts such as games, and in closed contexts such as gymnastics and dance where the quality of the movement is the criteria are much more problematic. The subjective nature and unreliability of the teachers assessment, the lack of standardization in conditions such as opponents and team members have all been used as arguments against assessment and examinations (Schools Council, 1977). There are many misconceptions about the nature of the subjective judgment of the teacher and consequently the reliability of such judgements. However, Aspin (1974) and Kirk (1984), in relation to the arts and aesthetics, which are regarded as being subjective, and McNamee (1990), in relation to PE more generally, have shown that assessments can be objectively made based on recognized criteria (see chapter 1). The evidence from GCSE would support this thesis. However the nature of the assessment and reliability of the teachers is not unique to PE. It applies equally to many other subjects, for example, those which use essay type work, particularly English, and of course, subjects like art and music. The standardization and reliability of teachers marks in GCSE generally have been called into question, though without real foundation, by the government's pronouncement of a maximum amount of course work as part of the GCSE. In this case, external examinations are seen to be a more objective and reliable standard than teachers' coursework and marking. Not only is this thinking misplaced, but in relation to PE practical performance, the problems are compounded in an assessment based on a one-off performance. PE teachers, through CSE and GCSE, have shown that they can meet the criticisms and difficulties, and what has been learnt from these situations will be of help in assessment in the National Curriculum.

Let us look at what is involved in assessing practical performance — the skills, processes and requirements of the teacher. Once the purposes and modes have been established, there are three main requirements:

(i)   To set the task and this involves planning and presentation.
(ii) To collect the evidence and this involves perception, interpretation and judgment.
(iii) To record the evidence.

Setting the Task

When I write here of setting the task this does not necessarily mean that it is set up for the specific purpose of assessment, it can be a normal class activity set up for teaching purposes because, as we have seen, assessment can and should be an integral part of teaching and learning situations. If the teacher is working towards assessment in the National Curriculum, the tasks should be set up with the End of Key Stage statements in mind. The teacher sets a task, for example, in games this may be an isolated skills practice, simulated-controlled games situation, or the full game context; in gymnastics this may be an isolated movement or a full performance, or a routine (sequence). Whatever it is, the task should conform to the principles set out in chapter 1. Figure 3 summarizes the principles related to setting up the task and dimensions influencing the control of the task. The teacher should ask him/herself the following questions:

Does the task assess what it is supposed to assess? (Is the task valid?)

Does the task allow me to assess what I want to assess? Does it assess the objectives? (Is the task valid?) (Is the task relevant?)

Is the task relevant to the standards of the pupils and styles of teaching? (Is the task relevant, appropriate?)

Does the task allow all the pupils the opportunity to show what they can do? The teacher also has the opportunity to control the task on a number of dimensions related to pupil and assessment needs – difficulty, variety, complexity and frequency and again these are questions which the teacher could ask him/herself.

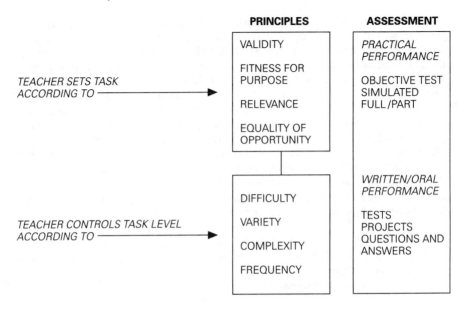

Figure 3: Requirements of a task used for assessment

Difficulty — Is the task too easy or too hard for the pupils? Can this skill be done in more or less different situations?

Variety — Can the skills be repeated in different situations?

Complexity — Can the skills be shown in more or less complex situations, for example, full games, skills in sequences?

Frequency — Can the skills be repeated?

The above list is clearly related to the task, they are not processes to be assessed, but they clearly influence the learning and levels of the performance of skills (see tables 9, p. 40 and 10, p. 46). It is not hard to set up an appropriate task in PE according to the main principles. I will come back to the issue of equality of opportunity. However, in games situations, it is not always so easy to get the levels of difficulty or complexity or variety of situations right for *all* standards of pupils at the same time, because there is usually a wide range of ability and performances. This is particularly so for those at the top or bottom of the performance range or for those pupils with special needs. This is because the teacher has to work with the group of pupils as a class and a different group cannot normally be 'imported' to control the opposition or team colleague standards. The GCSE has sometimes solved the problem at the top end of the performance range by using extra-curricular and club contexts, and 'A' level practical performance criteria refers to standards outside the immediate school. Although it looks an onerous task when assessment tasks are broken down like this as in figure 3, in actual fact, these principles and dimensions and all the above questions are ingredients of effective teaching and learning. It is just that teachers do not usually explicitly break down the task down like this, and with experience good teachers take much of it for granted in the teaching context and adjust the dimensions as required. However all teachers would benefit from reviewing their teaching and assessment from time to time, and then posing explicitly these questions to themselves.

Two other questions which have often been posed are;

Should the task be simulated?

Should the task be made objective? (that is use objective measurement).

There is no dispute on the question of objective measurement in relation to activities such as athletics and swimming, though, as we have seen, it seems justifiable and fair to also include assessment of techniques, water safety and life saving techniques. Some teachers do apply the objective measurement principle to games situations as part of the assessment and this does have some merit where it bears a close relationship to the games situation, for example, taking penalties in soccer, free shots in netball and basketball, serving in tennis. Outside the 'real' situation these tests do of course lack the pressure and authenticity of the 'real' game situation. The principle can be useful too in devising different levels of difficulty and complexity where a simulated and easier situation can be set up to assess selected skills based on objective scoring methods, for example, frequency counts. The West Midlands Examinations Board used objective scoring tests in all the games activities for part of the assessment in their CSE Mode 1 PE. The main advantage of this was of course standardization. However, it is significant that this practice was not continued in the Midland Examining Group's GCSE PE scheme. Presumably this is because it suffers from problems of artificiality, relevance and validity. The same charge can be levelled at isolating games situations or simulating them in simpler situations. However, this may be necessary to observe certain techniques and skills and to vary the difficulty level. For all levels of ability, this may be useful in teaching situations, for example, the taking away of the number of options available in a game situation, for controlling the situation for selected skills. For both teaching and assessing purposes it may be necessary to continue with this type of practice in order to provide lower ability pupils with some level of success and opportunities to develop. A teacher has to balance the demands of pupils' needs against the demands of the activity. It is a case of trading one principle against another. This is as important as providing pupils with the opportunity to show how they can perform in a full games situation with appropriate standards of opposition and team colleagues. What is at stake here is the principle of setting the task appropriate to the level of the pupils — relevance and opportunity.

Collecting the Evidence

Collecting the evidence will rely heavily on the teachers' observational skills. If the teacher is a poor (careless, inattentive, imperceptive) observer then an

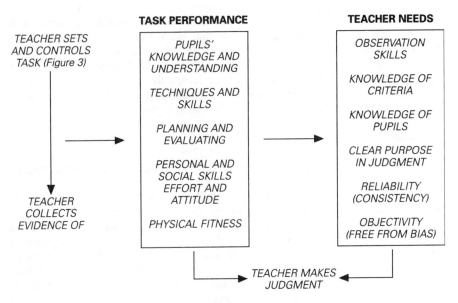

Figure 4:   Requirements of the teacher when assessing

accurate assessment cannot be made. In this case he/she is not likely to be a good teacher. The requirements of the teacher are shown in figure 4. The teacher must have:

Observational skills.
Detailed knowledge of the activity and criteria.
Clear purpose.

Then the assessment must be:

Objective (free from bias) and
Reliable (consistent) in the application of criteria (see chapter 1).

The evidence from the pupils is matched against an ideal of what is possible bearing in mind the pupils' development and experience. The criteria may be divided into four elements, technical, application of decision-making processes, physical and personal. Figure 5 shows these elements in an example of badminton. The teacher will find evidence in all four elements, though the difficulty in separating them has been noted in chapter 3. There are two aspects to each of the elements, firstly, the basic use of the element, and secondly, the effectiveness of the element in the full situation. The latter is not simple of course because there are also different elements of the context to consider in making a judgment, for example, the opponents and pressure of the situation. It is the teacher's interpretation of the context which is crucial of course, but if the requirements shown above and in figure 4 are adhered to, the assessment will be satisfactory. The

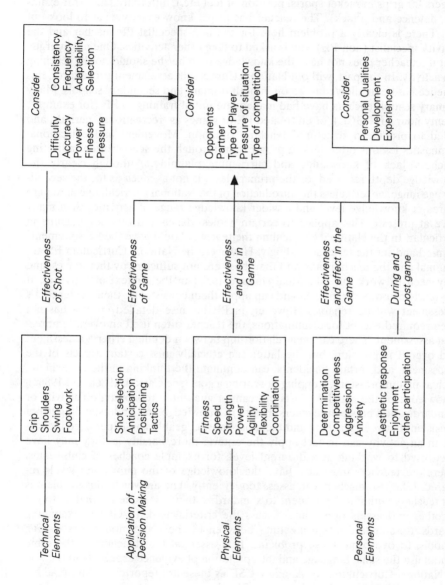

Figure 5: Model of criteria for assessment in a games situation (example from Badminton)

teacher will also judge the level of skill and performance, and will take into consideration factors outlined in figure 5.

The teacher needs to have a detailed knowledge of the activity in order to know the criteria and apply them, such as knowledge of techniques (position of fingers for grips in racket sports, position of feet etc.), different tactics (for example, defence and attack). The teacher has to get know exactly what to look out for. There is clearly a problem here for the non-specialist PE teacher and the activity specialist (non-PE) who is asked to take other activities. One might argue that if a teacher does not have the knowledge then he/she should not be teaching the activity. In the past, without National Curriculum assessment procedures, this practice has been allowed to go on in both primary and secondary schools. Many primary school teachers have had inadequate initial training in PE (for example, twenty hours in PGCE), often treated PE or games as 'recreational' periods, and failed to provide a structured teaching situation. Movement and educational gymnastics lessons often lacked progression through the school often indicating teachers' lack of knowledge and curriculum planning. Although clearly the knowledge depth required for the primary level is not as much as for the secondary age range, nevertheless the introduction of the National Curriculum will require a greater knowledge level and a wider knowledge range of activities than many have at present. This applies to certain games, dance and outdoor pursuits in particular. In the National Curriculum the teacher should have the ES statements in mind and set the tasks accordingly. However, the National Curriculum ES are minimal and the teacher may find that these are not sufficient by themselves, and may need to work out additional statements set in the context of activities. If the teacher knows the criteria and can apply them consistently then the teacher's assessment will be reliable. However, in PE because detailed criteria has not been required except for examinations, the teacher often used an overall impression assessment. There can be a relationship between detailed criteria assessment and overall impression, but the latter can crucially miss certain aspects of the assessment, and certain 'incidents' can dominate the thinking in the assessment, such as first impressions, stopping or scoring a goal (see Carroll, 1986b and 1986c). Knowledge of the activity assists but cannot guarantee reliability, objectivity or standardization between teachers. Depth of knowledge and understanding is not consistent between teachers and the most knowledgeable and experienced teachers in an activity can in fact apply the criteria more harshly as they may have been used to working at a different level, for example coaches of club teams. Therefore teachers must also have the knowledge of the pupils and levels required. Likewise teachers can assess too leniently. The answer to this problem is for teachers within a department to standardize their assessments, that is, to get together and assess pupils and discuss the criteria used. In GCSE, examining boards use standardization meetings between teachers and moderators visiting schools, to overcome these problems. It is essential that teachers in the same school use the same language and interpretation of evidence especially in relation to National Curriculum, ROA, and GCSE as these are reported to, and read by, other people. This can be taken care of by department and school policies. Idiosyncratic reporting will no longer do. Teachers are subject to their own biographies and experiences and they have their own frameworks, their own 'goggles on' (Kelly, 1955). These frameworks will guide their thinking. Superimposed on these 'frameworks' are teacher expectations of the pupils, which depend on their knowledge of pupils. Frameworks and expectations can unconsciously effect their judgments of pupils, for example, the 'halo effect' of social class and appearance, or the type of player they like (aggressive, creative). This is returned to in chapter 9.

There is certainly no shortage of evidence if the pupils get involved in the task. In fact, in the complex situation of all the children working, either at playing games, or different group activities in the gymnasium, there will be too much for the teacher to comprehend, cope with and use for teaching and assessment purposes. There must be selective attention on certain pupils and certain criteria. Difficulties can arise due to:

(a)   poor observational skills — carelessness, lack of attention to detail, not applying selective attention;

(b)   inappropriate task setting — levels of difficulty etc.;

(c)   'one off' examination of practical performance.

The teacher can do something about these in most circumstances. However, even if these difficulties are not present there are other issues to resolve such as:

1   How much evidence to collect. Is the single performance of a skill enough evidence? Can it be repeated? Can it be repeated in other situations? Although teaching in PE and the National Curriculum are not based on mastery learning, nevertheless the teacher will want to know and try to assess the level of mastery, for example:

Can it be performed once?
Can it be performed frequently?
Is it performed with poor or good technique?
Can it be performed in more difficult or complex situations?

It would be useful to work to a model as in table 9.

2   How far are other pupils, opponents or team members, affecting performance? Can these be changed to give other evidence?

3   How far is one criteria influencing another, for example; how can tactics be applied if skills and techniques are lacking? How can the range of skills be shown if tactics are not applied? What part do effort and personal qualities play in the performance?

Let us look at an example to illustrate these points, a pupil John playing badminton against Peter, who is the good 11-year-old mentioned in chapter 1. John knows that to win points against Peter he must serve high to the back of the court and make it difficult for Peter to attack the shuttle. However, John has not developed good enough technique to serve in this way; his serves fall short and are attacked. He must then adopt other tactics, such as short serves. Peter's technique allows him to serve high and effectively, but John's serves do not give Peter an opportunity to show his tactics in reply to good high effective serves. John is limited in technique and skill, and therefore cannot apply the appropriate tactics, but he may understand the tactics and this perhaps can be assessed orally. Peter needs to play against stronger opposition, who can serve high to show his full range of skills and tactics.

The teacher will also consider the amount of effort which John and Peter put into their performance. Carroll (1976a and 1976b) has indicated the importance of pupils' effort and the motivational dimension as the intervening variable between pupils' ability and performances. Indications of the amount of effort in relation to the ideal of pupils' performances reveal pupils' ability and potential. The greater the amount of effort the more likely potential ability is fulfilled, and the teacher can gauge from this progress and level of attainment. Furthermore, the motivational dimension is something the teacher feels he/she can do something about and is one measure of his/her success. Effort has always featured strongly on school reports and comes under personal qualities in ROA. Teachers do not seem to have much problem in recognizing effort and behavioural criteria (Carroll, 1976a and 1986c).

4   Making sense of and using the judgment — to assess progress, or comparison against others. The teacher asks questions such as:

> How does the performance compare with the pupil's previous performances?
> How does the pupil compare with others of the same age, physical development and same amount of experience of the activity?
> Is the pupil ready to go on to other tasks?

These of course relate to self, norm and criterion referencing and the reader is referred back to chapter 1. As shown in that chapter, these are not mutually exclusive and they can be used in conjunction with each other. The difficulty of moving solely to criterion referencing can be illustrated through NCC statements, and government actions. The NCC gave advice to teachers on the National Curriculum in PE (NCC, 1991). Whilst basically accepting the ES proposals on which teachers are to base their assessments, it goes on to state,

> It should be sufficient to judge a pupil's attainment during and at the end of the key stage in each area of activity in terms of a three point scale of below average, average and above average. (p. 12)

This shifts the assessment from the ES to the activities, and more importantly, from criterion to norm-reference assessment. The disadvantage is that pupils' performances are going to be compared to other childrens' rather than their own, and furthermore children can only progress to above average at the expense of others who will become below average. Although apparently withdrawn, the fact that the NCC made this recommendation in the first instance shows how difficult it is to get rid of the notion of norm referencing, and they made it in spite of the National Assessment arrangements being criterion reference in design. Also one can still read norm reference grading systems on records and reports. The Government too is guilty of encouraging norm-referencing with the publication of school and LEA National Curriculum test and GCSE results. This type of referencing appears to encourage and reinforce comparison with others as the important point of reference to the pupil and parents, a particular climate which is ego-orientated, competitive rather than cooperative. For the successful ones this may be motivating and give high self esteem, but in the case of the majority it may well be demotivating. (see Papaioannou, 1992). A learning environment and assessment system which emphasizes self-referencing, and mastery of tasks, may be more useful to the majority of the pupils. However, I am not so naive as to assume that pupils will not compare themselves to others whatever the system. Pupils will always do this, and the competitive environment in PE and in the context of games and athletics in particular, perhaps encourages this. However, all performances even educational gymnastics, dance, keep fit classes are open display situations and cannot avoid the comparative situation. It is the teachers' teaching-learning and assessment environment which may partly determine the influence.

Recording the Evidence

Recording the achievement and ROA will be discussed at greater length in chapter 7, but it must be mentioned here briefly for its part in the retaining and making known pupils' assessments and their part in involving the pupil. One of the problems for the teacher is the wealth of information and the other is the number of pupils. As we have seen the teacher cannot and must not try to assess everything, but even so all the evidence that is collected on each pupil cannot be remembered. Some form of recording by the teacher or pupil is essential in the interests of accuracy and to do justice to the pupil. Quite clearly this is a more difficult problem in PE than in a classroom subject and will be discussed in chapter 7.

Recording the evidence through video can be a very useful form of presentation, which can be used for teaching and pupil evaluation, such as the National Curriculum requirements for pupil evaluation. It would be particularly useful to show progress, and may be of particular interest to special needs groups in diagnosis. The advantage of this means of communication is that it could be related to cross-curricular skills if the pupils are themselves involved in the process of filming. However, a serious disadvantage is the time consuming nature and possible cost of this form of presentation.

Equality of Opportunity

The notion of equal opportunity for all pupils regardless of sex, ethnic groups, ability, social class, special needs should underpin all forms of assessment. However, there can be difficulties in meeting this principle because of prevailing ideologies and constraints in society. Take, for example, the gender issue, which has now been well commented upon in relation to PE (Evans, 1984 and 1989; Leaman, 1984; Talbot, 1990; Flintoff, 1990 amongst others) In these writings it is acknowledged that PE and sport not only portray masculine and feminine images and stereotypes but maintain ideas of gender differentiation about sports and leisure activities, and male power and hegemony (Flintoff, 1990). This argument about differentiation could also be applied to ethnicity, social class and disabilities. In the past equal opportunities had been largely ignored, but more recently the gender issue has been tackled by looking at class organization and curriculum, for example, the change from single sex to mixed groupings and opening up of previously single sex only activities to the other sex (Evans, 1989). In these instances teachers believe they have fulfilled the equal opportunities principle in relation to task setting, but as Evans (1989) and Flintoff (1990) observed this has not always been successful. In the assessment situation girls could be put at a severe disadvantage in say, for example, a mixed soccer or basketball situation, where their limited experience of the game may be immediately apparent, and where boys also dominate the teacher's attention. As Evans (1989) points out there are many similarities between the sexes and a person orientated approach to assessment is most appropriate. However, the teacher must be sensitive when differences should be taken into account, for example, strength, and how differences are reflected in performances. Evans (*ibid*) has articulated this argument well and finalizes it with a sentiment which I concur is apt in relation to assessment,

> In my view, any educational enterprise which has equality of the sexes high amongst its aims yet remains insensitive to the gender and sex differences which children bring to the classroom context is likely to be as ineffective in the mission as it is unrewarding and alienating for some girls and boys. (p. 87)

I have seen some examples of this insensitivity to sex differences in the past in CSE assessment where both girls and boys have been disadvantaged in different activity contexts. These seem more likely to occur in mixed sex groupings rather than single sex and where marks formalize the situation. No doubt where marks do not formalize the assessment the teacher's insensitivity and disadvantage to the pupil will still come through in the teaching-learning situation.

The same argument can be used in relation to pupils with special needs. There are wide ranging types of disability and these are going to effect performances in many different ways, and do present teachers with some difficulties in coping with these special needs in a large group. However, as the National Curriculum proposals point out strongly (DES, 1991b, appendix A) the activities in the curriculum should be available to these pupils in an integrated situation and where possible with little modification. However, clearly, the teacher must be sensitive to the special needs and how this affects performance, and must be taken into consideration in assessment. The person-orientated approach of ROA, where the achievements can be related to what they can be expected to achieve in view of their special needs is again the most appropriate. A norm-reference system is going to disadvantage this group of pupils.

The principle of equal opportunity applies to ethnic minority pupils as well. However, the different cultural traditions (includes all social and religious) of certain ethnic minority groups do often cause conflict, and also conflict with the principle of equal opportunity itself, at least from the European perspective. In an empirical study, Carroll and Hollinshead (1993a and 1993b) have shown how traditional approaches in PE, equal treatment and equal access have caused conflict between PE teachers and Muslim pupils, and between Muslim pupils and their parents and community. These conflicts revolve around the type of PE kit worn, changing, showers, mixed groupings, Ramadan (religious fast), and extra-curricular activities, and involved girls more than boys. The study showed that the way activities are presented rather than the activities themselves were causing the problems. Carrington and Williams (1988) and Carroll and Hollinshead (1993a and 1993b) support the view that equal opportunity cannot really exist for Muslim pupils without taking into consideration their religious commitments and demands. Quite clearly the way PE is presented is going to affect assessment. Fortunately by now most of these issues are well known to teachers with large ethnic minority group compositions in their schools and the issues can be resolved to a certain extent with negotiations and some compromise. However, it has been shown that Muslim communities give physical activity, sport and leisure activities a low priority in their culture (Fleming, 1991; Carrington and Williams, 1988; Carroll and Hollinshead, 1993a). Carroll (1993) has expressed concern that this may disadvantage these pupils in the National Curriculum because they may not be brought up to play and develop physical skills and sporting activities like their white English counterparts. This can lead to teachers' beliefs in low ability for particular groups and stereotyping. They may well be disadvantaged in the demand at the end of key stages for,

> involvement in physical activity for a healthy and enjoyable lifestyle, considering the use of community resources where appropriate (ES4). (DES, 1992)

A norm reference system such as first recommended by the NCC (1991) (already mentioned), is a case where the pupils would be disadvantaged. The issue of equal opportunities is complex, particularly where ethnicity and gender overlap. For example, Carroll and Hollinshead (1993a) have pointed out the difficulty of putting into operation the principle of equal opportunities for girls whilst at the same time accepting cultural diversity and the traditions of certain Muslim communities who have a different view of sex roles. However, teachers must be made aware of the issues, their own teaching and assessment practices and attempt to tackle their own prejudices if they exist.

When Will I Assess?

Discussing the issues in detail as I have done rather than taking a more simple pragmatic approach perhaps presents a more complicated picture than many teachers would wish and prompts the questions, 'when will I find time to assess?', 'when will I have time to consider all these issues?' The 'when' cannot be separated from the 'how'. The questions are partly answered in the foregoing text. The assessment of practical performance will take place in the teaching-learning situation as part of that process. If the purpose is formative, then it will also be used in that situation as feedback. If the purpose is summative, then it may take place at a specific time and it may well be used as a statement to show the stage or level the pupil is at, as in the End of Key Stages in the National Curriculum or in GCSE. This will require a comment or mark representing a level and will need to be recorded. It is the recording where perhaps there is more controversy over the amount of time involved. This is discussed in more detail in chapter 7.

However, now that there is a requirement to be more formal and more systematic in the assessment and recording, then teachers will have to decide when to put more effort into the assessment, and what stage will give them the best picture of the pupils' progress and learning. For instance, PE activities are often taught on a modular approach with blocks of lessons on particular activities. Should the main assessment come at the end of the block? This seems an obvious and pragmatic solution, but then should consideration be given to performances carried out during the course? If the activity is not taught again for another year, perhaps by another teacher, how will that assessment be used formatively? Quite clearly this method is most appropriate for summative assessments. However, in a year's time, it is quite likely that the performance in the activity will be lower without any practice, especially where growth and development have not made a profound influence. So even the last summative assessment may not give a true picture of the stage the pupil is at in any particular time. Quite clearly thought must be given as to how assessment at the end of the block of time can be used formatively. How assessment is to be done, how it relates to the curriculum must all be built into schemes of work. This way it is not seen as a discrete activity, and will not be seen as such a severe problem. Even examinations which have procedures influencing when assessment will take place should be built into the curriculum structure. It is a question of balancing the demands of assessment and the practicality of methods and procedures. There is no doubt that there is a time management problem here for teachers as well as an assessment problem. A school and departmental policy built into the curriculum structure will assist the teacher in the time management problem.

Chapter 5

How Can Theoretical Work be Assessed Satisfactorily?

This chapter would not have been appropriate a few years ago. However, as we have seen in chapter 2, the advent of the CSE brought theoretical work into PE which needed to be assessed in conventional ways. Theoretical work has since become established in GCSE PE syllabuses, and included as part of the National Curriculum, and has been discussed under 'cognitive objectives' in chapter 3. Traditionally theoretical work was not a demand of PE teaching, so it is not surprising that PE teachers had not been trained in the use of conventional techniques of assessment. There are many teachers of all subjects in schools who also have no formal training in assessment techniques either. All teachers have gone through schooling and are in fact successes of the examination system. They are also experts in their subjects so perhaps it is often taken for granted that they know how to set and mark different types of questions and examination papers very well. However, in fact, specific expertise is required to devise suitable questions and mark schemes over and above the expertise in the subject. It is my experience through INSET and examination moderating that many PE teachers lack this expertise. Before I examine the general requirements of specific assessment techniques, I will look at the technique requirements related to objectives and knowledge component of the GCSE and the National Curriculum.

The same basic principles are required for an effective assessment of theoretical work as well as practical work (see figures 4 and 5 and chapter 1). The task must adhere to the principles, but is now in either written or oral form, and the teachers' criteria is purely in the cognitive domain. The problem with selecting oral methods is the time consuming nature of individual answering and, like physical performance, there is no permanent record unless recorded. The advantage of the written word is that it can be assessed outside the lesson in a more considered way and is a permanent record. The same basic requirements of the teacher are also essential to theoretical assessment as in practical assessment (see figure 5 and chapter 1), but the skills required shift from observational to question and answer and traditional examining techniques.

Cognitive Objectives in the National Curriculum and GCSE

Table 12 shows the National Curriculum End of Key Stage Statements which require a cognitive assessment and these have been related to suggested forms of

Table 12: National Curriculum ES and cognitive assessments

Statements	Means of Communication	Type of questions or Teaching style
KS1. Describe what they and others are doing.	Oral in practical situation.	Objective questions.
Recognize the effects of physical activity on their bodies.	Oral in practical situation.	Objective questions.
KS2. Evaluate how well they and others perform and behave against criteria suggested by the T. and suggest ways of improving.	Oral in practical situation. To teacher. To other pupils.	Objective questions. Reciprocal style. Problem solving.
... understand the effects of exercise on the body.	Oral in practical situation.	Objective questions.
KS3. Understand and evaluate how they and others have achieved what they set out to do, appreciate strengths and weaknessess and suggest ways of improving.	Oral in practical situation. To teacher. To other pupils. Written.	Objective & structured questions. Reciprocal style. Problem solving.
KS4. Prepare, carry out and monitor personal programmes for a healthy and enjoyable lifestyle, considering the use of community resources.	Written and practical. Oral in practical situation. To teacher To other pupils.	Objective & structured questions. Project/assignment. Report to group. Problem solving style.

communication and to an example of the assessment technique. It is suggested that in many of these assessments the appropriate method is oral in the practical situation, and this is particularly so for the primary age group, where the most appropriate question technique suggested is the short objective answer. It is emphasized that the practical performance predominates at all stages, but particularly so at the primary age and that the assessment is continuous and takes place as part of the normal lessons in the practical situation. The time consuming nature of oral communication must be managed properly. The requirement of pupil evaluation in assessment would suggest a teaching style of working in pairs and commenting/evaluating performance in pairs. In Mosston's terms this is called reciprocal teaching, where one pupil acts as teacher, the other as pupil and this is where the pupils assess each other and diagnose the skills and techniques (Mosston, 1986). The teacher then goes round, observing and talking to teacher-pupils as required. The problem comes in making a note of how far each pupil is good at this evaluating, applying the right criteria etc. However, this method does require some adjustment and practice for the pupils as many do take some time to adjust to the teacher-evaluator's role. It is particularly difficult for many young children as it requires knowledge of the technique, skills and the activity. Many children can verbalize the evaluation and apply the criteria but have difficulty in the written form, as has been required for GCSE.

It can be noted that table 12 shows that the written form is more appropriate at the later stages where a greater knowledge and understanding is required. This knowledge in POS KS4 (DES, 1991b, 8.86 and 1992) is a good example and has similarities with GCSE and perhaps should be assessed in the same way.

Table 13: *Showing objectives, knowledge, methods and techniques of assessment in GCSE*

Examination	Objectives	Methods	Techniques
GCSE	Knowledge and understanding of Physical (sports science) Social (issues, organization) (not LEAG) Activities (not NEA)	Written Exam. (unseen)	Objective question — 1 word, short answer Multiple choice (LEAG) Matching block (SEG) Structured question Open ended (NEA, SEG)
	Research, Analysis Selected area (NEA)	Project	Variety of techniques Observation Practical involvement Collect data Written report

So, structure and functions of the human body could be tested by short answer, objective testing. The monitoring and recording of fitness could be done in the practical situation, but the recording of the practical sessions, as in science laboratory work, would be appropriate and useful information for the pupil. This would show the teacher the work the pupil has completed and whether it has been understood. The statements of attainment related to leisure, community and vocational opportunities in the area might well be assessed through a small project, asking them to find out information and then report it to the class. This may even be done on a group basis.

Table 13 shows the types of objectives and knowledge, the methods of assessment and techniques (types of questions) employed in the GCSE. An examination of the papers reveals that there is a lot of similarity between the different GCSEs on the type of questions generally, although there are differences in format and structure. The majority of questions are objective, one word or short answer questions and demand factual recall or description. They take the form of listing, sentence completion, multiple choice, matching blocks etc. This is particularly so for the physical basis of performance — anatomy and physiology etc and to a slightly lesser extent knowledge and understanding of sport in society, and of physical activity.

It can be useful here to utilize Bloom's Taxonomy of Objectives (Bloom, 1956) and Peel's Level of Understanding (Peel, 1971) (table 10, p. 46). These should not be looked at as strict hierarchies of knowledge or processes but as types of cognitive activity as responses. Some indeed are more difficult than others, but in a given context, it is not necessary to have reached one level before another level can be operated. Young children can respond to what can be described as the later levels to a limited extent, as indeed they are being asked to do so for example with evaluation at Key Stage 2. A lot may depend on the context and the way the information is taught and requested, for example, Key Stage 1 asks children 'to recognize the effects of physical activities on their bodies' (NCC, 1991; DES, 1991b and 1992). This is a 'cause and effect' relationship which the pupils are being asked to understand, and may involve the Peel's explainer 3 level (Peel, 1971) or Bloom's application level (Bloom, 1956). Because of the practical context of the situation, a young child may well be able to understand the principle and give the teacher a response.

Table 14: Cognitive processes linked to question difficulty from Pollitt et al. (1985)

Explaining
Generalizing
Selection of Data
Identifying a Principle
Application of a Principle

Question Difficulty and Cognitive Processes

In an analysis of selected subjects in Scottish 'O' level, Pollitt *et al* (1985) suggested processes linked directly to question difficulty rather than a predetermined hierarchy, but which were generalisable across subjects (table 14). These are not a hierarchy but do bear a relation to Bloom's and Peel's categorizations. Pollitt *et al* stated that these processes 'did not always coincide with what the question appeared to ask, as with the demands of the mark scheme' (p. 75). This suggests that the mark scheme may indicate different demands than the question, which surely has a lesson for the teacher and examiner, that is, to always ensure the process demands of the mark scheme coincide with that of the question. So if we return to the GCSE, there are a few questions which do demand comprehension, application, analysis and evaluation, or the explainer levels in Peel's theory. Of course one must look at the objectives and the weighting carefully before one decides whether they are fulfilling the demands of the syllabus. The issues are: (i) whether the questions meet their objectives (whether the examiner had asked the right type of questions and in appropriate quantities); and (ii) whether the form they have chosen (for example, the written) is the most appropriate for the type of knowledge and understanding. The examination board's syllabuses refer to the 'Knowledge' and 'Understanding' but, apart from a further use of 'apply' in two instances, exactly what this means is not stated. Examiners and PE teachers usually refer to understanding as 'application of knowledge' and 'knowing what something means', or 'knowing what the effects of something are' (Bloom's comprehension, application levels). There is evidence to show that this is being tested by the questions. However there is much less emphasis on analysis and evaluation and Peel's category 4 level. If one looks at the syllabuses one can see that these processes may relate only to a particular component of the syllabus, for example,

> assess, interpret and evaluate situations related to a selected range of games ... (LEAG);

and again,

> ... analysis of performance (MEG);

and

> ... analysis through observation (SEG)

This usually refers to the performance component. Most boards (except NEA) have chosen to answer these by written questions in examination papers as well as during practical performance, and these are usually divided into sections of 'physical activities' and 'sports', and a candidate selects the activities and answers all the questions relating to a specific activity. However some of the papers show that supposedly equivalent questions in different sections (activity-related) are not evenly demanding, for example, no evaluation required in some sections but demanded in others. If one looks at all the papers there are few questions which demand an evaluation (judgment by candidates, weighing up evidence and decision making evaluation) such as in,

What are the advantages and disadvantages of . . .

but even here they could be learnt without having to work them out for themselves. This point is important now with the advent of the National Curriculum which demands evaluation.

There are a few open-ended and essay-type questions, for example, in the NEA papers. However, the difficulty of marking essay-type questions is well known and the need to standardise the marking is essential. To do this exam boards develop mark sheets of points to look for, which become objective — so much so in fact that one wonders what is the point of asking an open-ended question (see Sheridan, 1974; and MacIntosh, 1974). Why ask to 'discuss' when a list of points will elicit the same marks. Moreover the pupils are not usually told this. One can readily see the advantage in the types of questions which do predominate — the short objective and highly structured questions. These have objectivity and reliability between examiners and are easily checked.

Many of the questions ask the candidate to describe a technique, which often needs breaking down, but often pupils do have difficulty in making these descriptions of a practical movement without seeing it in front of them. Many pupils may not be able to do a technique/skill well or effectively but they may know 'how to do' it and what should be done. But whether they can do it or not many pupils would probably explain it better orally and probably the most appropriate form would be in a practical situation. Time is the enemy here, of course. However, analysis and evaluation could take part in the practical situation as it is in 'A' level PE oral, possibly working in pairs or groups within coursework. This will show what pupils 'know, understand and can do' better than the present system. The use of video is an alternative method.

Projects are the best way of testing investigatory techniques, interpretation of findings and evaluating the work. However, they suffer from problems of variety and therefore standardisation problems. However, it is possible to lay down broad guidelines for presentation and criteria for assessment as the NEAB GCSE has done (see chapter 6).

Setting Questions

I am not going to write in detail about how to write the different types of questioning as that has been done far better elsewhere and teachers are advised to consult these texts (MacIntosh, 1974; Satterly, 1989). However, I am going to

Table 15: Types, examples of question difficulty and control requirements

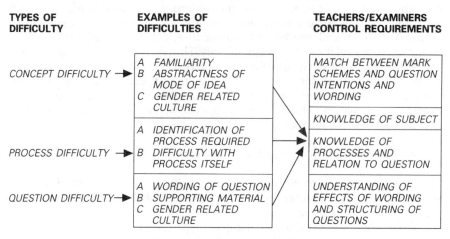

TYPES OF DIFFICULTY	EXAMPLES OF DIFFICULTIES	TEACHERS/EXAMINERS CONTROL REQUIREMENTS
CONCEPT DIFFICULTY →	A FAMILIARITY B ABSTRACTNESS OF MODE OF IDEA C GENDER RELATED CULTURE	MATCH BETWEEN MARK SCHEMES AND QUESTION INTENTIONS AND WORDING
		KNOWLEDGE OF SUBJECT
PROCESS DIFFICULTY →	A IDENTIFICATION OF PROCESS REQUIRED B DIFFICULTY WITH PROCESS ITSELF	KNOWLEDGE OF PROCESSES AND RELATION TO QUESTION
QUESTION DIFFICULTY →	A WORDING OF QUESTION B SUPPORTING MATERIAL C GENDER RELATED CULTURE	UNDERSTANDING OF EFFECTS OF WORDING AND STRUCTURING OF QUESTIONS

point to some issues to bear in mind because many PE teachers will find they do need to do some testing now. Clearly this is most useful for those taking GCSE, where, to give pupils their best chance of success, they will have to get them to answer practice papers. Whilst, obviously, the teacher can give past papers, at the present time these are limited in number, and marks schemes are not always available. The teacher might find it useful to devise some of his/her own and build up a bank of suitable questions. With the advent of the National Curriculum as we have seen there are areas of knowledge and understanding which might be assessed through written work, for example, knowledge of structure and functions of the human body (objective questions), knowledge of rules of games activities (objective questions), understanding of tactics (structured questions), knowledge of community leisure and opportunities (project, open-ended questions).

Pollitt *et al* (1985) suggested that candidates' problems in answering questions fell into three categories:

(i) Subject or concept difficulty, where particular concepts or areas of the subject may be more or less difficult, which may be due to familiarity or the abstractness of the idea.

(ii) Process difficulty, which is not concerned with the subject matter, but with the operations a pupil has to undertake, for example, recall, applying knowledge, analysis, apply principles.

(iii) Question difficulty, which is related to the wording of the question itself, for example, the way in which it directs attention to a particular response, or whether the structure gives a level of support or not.

Table 15 illustrates these difficulties. Pollitt *et al* (*ibid*) also pointed out that illegitimate difficulty did exist, which was where the question sought to test something, but unintentionally tested something else as well, or where the mark scheme did not coincide with the questioners intentions. This research has lessons for every teacher and examiner and suggests questioners should adhere to basic principles:

> ... that the setting of good examination questions depends on gaining control of the processes involved in answering the questions set; controlling the outcome space' and the way that candidates come to define it for themselves; and ensuring a match between this and the examiner's own intended outcome space as explicit in the marking scheme. This control depends partly on an intimate knowledge of the subject to be examined as it is taught, but also on an understanding of the crucial effects of the wording and structuring of question papers on candidates' performance. (*ibid*, p. 83)

If pupils are to show what they know, understand and can do, it is essential that those setting questions have the control as indicated in the above passage. One can read chief examiners' reports of GCSE examinations where comments such as,

> ... proved ambiguous for others

> ... many misunderstood the requirements ...

> There was confusion over ...

are common. In these instances it is very often the examiner who has not gained adequate control over the processes and wording of questions. A couple of different examples from GCSE PE will illustrate this control element.

Question related to tennis

> How would the movement of the racquet head change when 1) the ball is played at shoulder height? 2) the ball is played at knee height? (LEAG, paper 2, 1991)

In the report the examiner stated that 'many misunderstood the requirements', and the mark scheme showed the answers required were,

> (i)   Forward and downward movement or face closed.
> (ii) Forward and upward movement or face open.

Perhaps it is not surprising that the requirements were misunderstood. The candidates may have been uncertain about what was meant by 'racquet head change' and it would have been better worded:

> Describe the movement of the racquet head when ...

However, the answer to this depends on a number of factors, position on court, type of shot received, the type of shot being played, for example, topspin, slice or flat, and possibly even the height of the person. Just to take one of these, the type of shot/stroke. If it is to be basically a topspin then the movement of the racket head is from down to up as it goes forward, whilst if it is sliced then the movement is from up to down in its forward movement with face open. So in actual fact either answer is acceptable for both parts.

In another question in a paper belonging to another examination board, candidates are asked to suggest an exercise using 'medicine balls' in a circuit amongst other equipment. The examiner stated 'surprisingly, many candidates did not know what a medicine ball was and many did not match up a suitable exercise to the stated station' (SEG, 1991). This is not too surprising to me as many schools do not have medicine balls and many candidates will not have seen one. This clearly relates to concept/subject difficulty where candidates are not familiar with the term. The question is whether 'medicine balls' are regarded as central or peripheral to the syllabus and whether they should be familiar with the term.

A more demanding question asks,

> You are about to embark on a programme in preparation for a distance run. What aspects of fitness would be required, how would you measure your progress and what other factors may be important during your preparation?

Amongst the examiner's comments were

> This question was very badly answered. There was poor knowledge of 'training principles', although many candidates wrote on components of fitness, very few candidates extended their thought beyond their own experience. (SEG, 1991)

What may have happened here is that candidates were 'directed' by the 'you' to utilize their own experience which would have been limited. It is noticeable that the candidates were able to say something on fitness components and this was specifically mentioned in the question whereas the 'training principles' were not. What this question demanded was not only some facts about preparation for a distance run, but applying some principles in monitoring progress. Candidates have to put the question and answer in forms they can deal with (see Pollitt *et al*, 1985) and in this question the 'you' helps them to do this, but the abstractness of the principles of training was clearly beyond a lot of the candidates. If they had known them, a restructuring of the question may have helped them.

A comment by the same examiner that another question elicited responses related to the candidates' own school experience illustrates how candidates translate questions and answers into forms they can deal with, and cannot meet the 'higher' process demands of the examiners. Teachers may not have given the pupils sufficient information and principles to apply in particular parts of the syllabus, but it is also likely they have not shown them how these type of questions are to be answered. Merely doing a practice paper is not always sufficient.

To test knowledge of syllabus content, the most appropriate technique is the short answer objective test. This can be given orally and in written form and is easily marked, even by pupils. They give equal opportunities to poor writers and communicators as well as good ones and does not mark other abilities such as verbal. External examination boards go through a process of setting, revising editing and checking with comments by revisers and committees of teachers and yet, as we have seen, ambiguous questions can still be set. Teachers need to go through a similar careful, but of necessity, simpler process, and it would pay teachers to get another teacher in the department or experienced teacher from another department to go through them and make comments. It can be a good idea to ask the pupils themselves how they interpret questions. Sometimes different formats are used to give variety but also to give equal opportunities to all candidates to show what they can do. However, bringing in formats such as true/ false, multiple choice or other prompts also allows the pupil to guess. Writing multiple choice is not as easy as it seems because the distractors must not be too irrelevant. They must appear as if they could be correct to pupils who do not know the correct answer.

Short objective questions can only assess factual recall of content and cannot get at understanding and the 'higher' processes. Structured and open-ended questions are required for these purposes. The problem with the open-ended essay type of question, such as, 'Discuss . . .', 'Write about . . .' is that, on the surface, they allow the pupil to answer in his/her own way to give the widest choice, but they do not give enough guidance for many pupils. They would be better with a more structured version, or, one with suitable prompts or leads. The teacher or examiner has his/her own 'frameworks' and is looking for particular answers, which the pupil has to guess or 'work out' what they are. The pupils' 'framework' and relevances may be different. Keddie's research is a good illustration of the differences and 'frameworks' between 'A' and 'C' stream pupils and how teachers accepted 'A' stream pupil answers as 'right' because they coincided with their own 'frameworks', whilst rejecting the 'C' stream answers as 'wrong' (Keddie, 1971). Yet seen through a different 'framework' and experience these 'C' answers were not necessarily wrong. It was the pupils' experiences and 'frameworks' which was being deemed invalid by the teachers. One might think that the 'discuss' type questions would automatically allow the better pupils to show application, analysis, and evaluation. However, they might choose to state and apply facts, to describe rather than analyze and evaluate, if these processes are not more specifically stated. If these 'higher' order skills are required a more structured question to elicit these processes would in all probability be better. These type of questions (open-ended and semi-structured) can be time consuming to set and mark. However they should be seen as an integral part of teaching and learning, to test understanding and give feedback to pupils in formative assessment, and not just as summative and examination questions.

What is important is that different types of questions are used over a period of time or in any one course so that the different objectives and processes can be assessed, and pupils of different abilities can be seen to be given a fair chance.

Equal Opportunities

Equal opportunities was discussed in relation to practical performance in the last chapter, and it was suggested that teachers must be sensitive to differences where appropriate. The same applies to cognitive performance. In recent years there has been much discussion of differences in performance in the majority of subjects between boys and girls, and between ethnic minority groups and the white British majority group. Some of these differences have been shown to be due to test bias either in the form of the content and context of the questions where the wording is more relevant or 'friendly' to a particular group, or, in the type of questions, for example, multiple choice or essay. The EOC in TGAT (EOC, 1988) and Gipps (1990) summarize some of the research findings on these issues. Although all this work is related to other subjects and not PE, it does have lessons for every subject on the way questions and test papers should be set to avoid bias.

The evidence of the Assessment and Performance Unit (APU) tests shows that girls do better than boys at reading and writing at ages of 11 and 15, in mathematics, 'girls do less well at measurement and spatial topics, applied and practical maths', and in science boys outperformed girls at applying concepts and interpreting data and reading information (*ibid*). Generally public examination results show boys do better in maths and science subjects whilst girls do better in the humanities. The school itself has an influence on these results and so does exposure to subjects (*ibid*). Other evidence suggests that boys do better than girls in multiple choice questions, but girls do better in free response and essay type questions, and the content of the question can be boy or girl friendly (EOC, 1988). Murphy (1989) suggests that boys see a problem differently than girls and that they are more likely to abstract the problem from the context whilst girls focus on the totality of the problem and the clues.

The research on ethnic minority group performances showed the West Indian children performed less well than the British white population (DES, 1985). Later more sophisticated studies have shown the effect of the school as an important variable (Gipps, 1990). Clearly language, where English is not the first language at home, can cause considerable difficulties at first and result in lower performance and expectations. The later research shows that differences between groups are not as large as they used to be (*ibid*). However, there appears to have been little research work carried out on ethnic culture bias in the way it has been tackled in relation to gender.

What does all this mean for PE? Clearly the lessons should be applied to eliminate bias in the assessment. In relation to content there is no evidence to indicate examples of girl friendly, boy friendly, or cultural group friendly questions, save the obvious ones of activities which are predominately played by one particular group. This is easily avoided by giving alternatives. What must apply here is the principle of equal difficulty, same types of questions and same types of processes demanded in the alternatives. In relation to the type of question, the evidence suggests that neither multiple choice, which favours boys and free choice which favours girls, should predominate in the weightings overall. It would appear that boys are more likely to do well on science content components of the syllabus and where demands are made in terms of applying science concepts, measurement etc, so may do better on the sports science papers (particularly as they are dominated by closed and multiple choice type questions) and science type projects. On the other hand, it would appear that girls would do better on the social science component and humanities type project. There is no evidence for these assertions in PE. An analysis of GCSE papers and GCSE results which would have given us this information has not been made on this basis. Teachers and examiners should perhaps be aware of these possibilities and design their tests and questions to take into account of this possibility. Only experience will tell us whether it is correct.

So far we have answered teachers' basic questions about assessment — the *Why, What, How and When*. However, there are many issues remaining relating to examinations, recording, and the National Curriculum. These will be explored in the next three chapters.

Chapter 6

Issues in Examinations and Accreditation

We have already seen in chapter 2 how examinations became part of the PE scene, and how these appear to have gained a strong footing both on the academic and the vocational fronts. There have been other forms of accreditation and certification, such as governing bodies of sport award schemes, which were popular in some quarters before examinations and which have proliferated in recent years and units of accreditation of various types which have been prompted by TVEI and CPVE. Figure 6 lists these different types of courses and forms of accreditation, and they cater for academic/non-vocational and vocational routes into further and higher education and employment. It can be readily seen that not all the courses are PE or even sport, and the vocational route has broader courses into recreation and leisure. This has been a natural sequel particularly for FE colleges, where sport has been seen as a natural part of the recreation and leisure industries, and PE teachers and lecturers have played a strong part in this development. Brief mention will be made of the latest developments in this sphere, but the bulk of this chapter will be spent on courses and issues more directly related to PE such as GCSE as I do not want to be sidetracked into the leisure field as that is a vast area in its own right.

GCSE Administration

The GCSE was set up to replace the GCE 'O' level and CSE examinations, but it was not just an amalgamation of two examinations. There were substantial changes, for example, the idea of criterion referencing and fitting in with national and subject specific criteria. Brown (1990) even goes so far as to suggest that, along with National Curriculum testing, the aim was to raise standards and to be more accountable, and that in combination 'they were among the most radical and significant (changes) of the twentieth century' (p. 79). Together the GCSE and the National Curriculum were much more of a national plan for the curriculum, examining and assessing in schools than had ever existed before.

The GCSE is administered by examining groups, which were formed by an association of the GCE and CSE boards, in which there had to be one of each type. In England four groups were set up, whilst the Welsh Board (WJEC) and the Northern Ireland Board (NISEAC), which had previously administered both

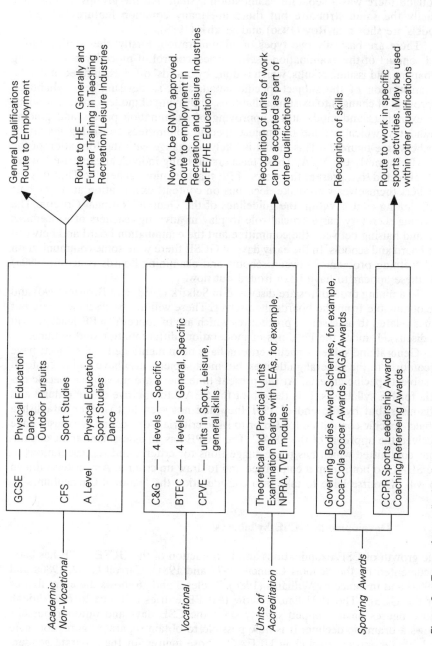

Figure 6: Types of accreditation, function and career routes

the GCE and CSE, took over the GCSE in those countries respectively, and in Scotland there was a separate examination system. All the groups do not have exactly the same structure but there are many common features. Different models are shown in Roy (1986) and Selkirk (1988).

There are basically two types of administration. Firstly, the administration and conduct of the examination itself, entries, control of procedures, processing of papers, and issuing results, which is done by boards' officials, and secondly, the administration of the subject-specific detail, such as devising new syllabuses, approving of changes to existing syllabuses, approving of mode 2 and 3s, appointing examiners and moderators, approving of examination papers and grading candidates, which is done by subject specific committees consisting mainly of teachers (see figure 7). This model is likely to change with the formation of the NEAB, formerly the NEA. These teachers do bring individual expertise but are also expected to represent the views of PE teachers more generally. Thus it is the teachers themselves who make decisions on content, examination arrangements etc., as long as it is within the guidelines of the General National Criteria. The servicing secretary has a crucial role to play in advising teachers of procedures etc. and liaising between the committee and the examination board and between the board and schools. In the early days of GCSE there were some communication and teething problems between schools and examining boards (Carroll, 1990a) but these appear to have been ironed out now.

Examining procedures are discussed in Selkirk (1988) and Brown (1990) and are obtainable from the boards themselves. These will not be discussed here but issues related to assessment procedures which are of concern to PE teachers will be discussed under the headings of moderation, differentiation and grading.

General and subject-specific criteria have been mentioned. All subjects have to conform to the general guidelines, but most subjects also have had to conform to subject-specific criteria. At the present time there are no subject-specific criteria for PE syllabuses. It is the job of the SEAC to approve of the criteria and syllabuses, but by the end of 1991 they had not seen fit to either establish a subject-specific committee for PE or to issue criteria. All existing syllabuses have received the approval of the SEAC. The BCPE has an assessment and examinations committee which has made suggestions for criteria and representations to the SEAC to both form a committee and to draw up criteria. Any criteria drawn up will of course have to take into consideration the National Curriculum.

Development: GCSE Syllabuses

The growth of CSE examinations and introduction of the GCSE in PE has been documented by the Schools Council (1977 and 1981), Carroll (1982, 1986a and 1990a) and in dance by Williams (1986). Tables 3 and 16 shows the entry figures for the GCSE. The 1992 figures show that PE entries continue to rise, though dance figures have dropped slightly since the CSE days and outdoor pursuits shows a dramatic decline. It is now possible to obtain separate figures for male and female entries. Excluding ULEAC, whose figures for the separate genders were not available, what is striking from table 16 is that approximately twice as many males as females took the PE examination, and about eighteen times the number of girls as boys took the dance examination. Whether these figures are

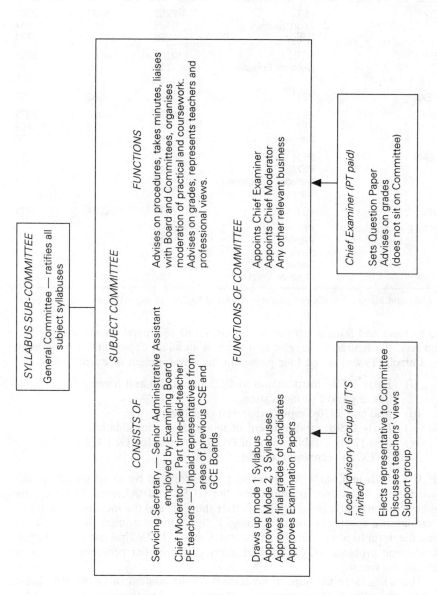

Figure 7: NEA model of subject committee and its functions

Table 16: Entry figures for GCSE 1992

Examination Group	Title	Total No	Male	Female
MEG	PE1	7252	5003	2249
	Sport Studies	486	339	147
	Dance	769	39	730
NEAB	PE1	10130	6565	3565
	Outdoor Pursuits	119	99	20
		1268	72	1196
NISEAC	PE1	922	566	356
SEG	PE1	10620	6947	3673
	PE2	598	429	169
	Dance	286	12	274
ULEAC	PE1	10721	**	**
	PE2/3	49		
	Outdoor Education	18		
	Dance	411		
WJEC	PE1	3305	2094	1211
TOTALS	PE1	42950		
	PE2/3	647		
	Sport Studies	486		
	Dance	2754		
	Outdoor Pursuits	137		

** Male and Female figures not available from the ULEAC at the time of going to press.

due to male and female interest in the GCSE or real pupil choice is not clear. However, the figures do suggest that there is an equal opportunities issue here.

Carroll (1986a) noted four phases in the development of examinations.

(i) Early 1970s: introduction to CSE (mode 3s) and ironing out difficulties, a period of innovation.
(ii) Mid/late 1970s: rapid expansion of schemes.
(iii) Early 1980s: establishment of mode 1s — consolidation.
(iv) Mid-1980s: establishment of GCSEs 'A' levels CGLI 481 syllabus and BTEC in recreation and leisure.

The late 1980s and early 90s have been characterized by rapid growth in the academic-non-vocational examinations, the GCSE and 'A' level. There clearly has been a dramatic take-up of GCSE after the CSE and the increase in numbers of entries and centres is still continuing. If this trend continues then it will become the norm to offer a GCSE PE course. Carroll (1990a) has commented upon introduction problems of GCSE, and many of the earlier problems have been met and overcome.

There is a large measure of agreement on the content of GCSE PE. Table 17 shows the main content, percentage weighting and methods of assessment for the GCSE syllabuses. Titles of components of the syllabus vary considerably but the content has a lot of similarities. To overcome this problem, in table 17, the heading 'sports science' refers to content covering anatomy, physiology, health-related fitness, psychology of skill, and the physical basic of performance. The heading 'social' refers to organization and participation, contemporary issues in

Table 17: Assessment weightings in GCSE and 'A' level

	Practical	Theoretical	Project
LEAG (ULEAC) GCSE PE	5 activities × 12% = 60% (30% continuous. 30% Exam)	Written Examination Sports Science 20% K & U Activities 20%	
MEG GCSE PE	4 activities × 12.5% = 50% (continuous assessment)	Written Examination Sports Science. Social. 30% K & U Activities. 20%	
NEA (NEAB) GCSE PE	4 activities × 12.5% = 50% (continuous assessment)	Written Examination Sports Science. Social 30%	In Selected Area 20%
SEG GCSE PE	5 activities × 10% = 50% (continuous assessment)	Written Examination K & U Activities + Sports Science, Social 50% *for Grades C–G* or value reduced to 30% + paper (essays) 20% *for Grades A–G.* *For Grades A–G*	
WJEC GCSE PE	4 activities × 15% = 60%	K & U Activities 12% Sports Science 28%	
NISEAC GCSE PE	4 activities × 15% = 60%	Sports Science. Social 40% or Extended Paper.	
AEB 'A' Level PE	2 activities × 15% = 30%	Written Examination core disciplines 35% 2nd yr options 35% core disciplines 40% 2nd yr options 40%	
'A' Level Sport Studies	None		Project 20%

81

Table 18: Categories of physical activities in GCSE with pupils' selection options

LEAG (ULEAC)	3 groups. 1 Games 2 Racket Sports 3 Individual Activities. Select 1 from each group + 2 others = 5.
MEG	2 groups. 1 Major Games 2 Other Activities. Select 2 from group 1 but not more than 2 marked * + 2 others = 4.
NEA (NEAB)	2 groups. 1 Games 2 Individual Activities. Select 1 from each + 2 others = 4.
SEG	3 groups. 1 Games 2 Net/Racket games 3 Individual Activities. Select 1 from each group + 2 others = 5.
NISEAC	3 groups. 1 Team 2 Individual Activities 3 Striking Games. Select 1 from each group + 1 other = 4.
WJEC	3 groups. 1 Gymnastics/Dance 2 Team Games 3 Individual Activities. Select 1 from each + 1 other = 4.

sport and PE, sport within society, whilst 'Knowledge and Understanding' (K&U) of activities refers to rules, laws, techniques, tactics and anything else related to a specific activity. The main differences between the syllabuses are that: LEAG does not include anything on 'sport and society' or 'local organization and participation'; MEG includes 'acquisition of skills', and has nothing on 'local participation'. The main difference in practical content is in the categorisation and range of activities available (see table 18). There is little difference in the content of the physical activities themselves. Some of the groups allow other activities on approval of a submission of a syllabus by the centre or centres. For a full range of activities in each syllabus the syllabuses need to be consulted.

Table 17 gives the weightings by percentage in the assessment of mode 1s in PE. For practical performance assessment, all boards use course work assessment by the teacher with teacher standardization and/or external moderation. It is usually left up to the teacher when the practical assessment takes place, whether it is continuous during an activity or at a specific time in the course, but the period of moderation is stipulated by the board. LEAG is the only board which also includes a practical examination — it divides its 60 per cent practical performance into 30 per cent course work by teachers and 30 per cent as a final examination. Many PE teachers would argue that a final examination is not the most appropriate method of assessment for practical performance, relying on one occasion only and the context of the opponents and team members available, and possibly weather etc. It may not give the pupils the opportunity to show what they can actually do. Moderation is covered later under that particular heading.

The main difference in the theoretical assessment, apart from small differences in weightings, is that the NEA has a study worth 20 per cent (discussed later) and SEG has a differentiated paper, and this is discussed under 'differentiation' later in this chapter.

Theoretical-Practical Balance

PE has been traditionally a practical subject. In Kane's (1974) and Underwood's (1983) large-scale surveys, there is no mention of theoretical work and in Carroll's

(1982) CSE survey no school reported theoretical work in non-CSE PE. No record of theory work existed yet theoretical work quickly established itself in CSE schemes. Carroll (1982) reported that all four mode 1 schemes available at that time gave between 40–60 per cent to theoretical assessment, and that 72 per cent of the mode 3 schemes (233 in number) weighted theory 40–60 per cent with 26 per cent giving more to theory. Table 17 shows that this has been carried through to GCSE with LEAG, WJEC and NISEAC weighting theory at 40 per cent whilst the other three (NEA, MEG, SEG) all give 50 per cent to theory. It is interesting to speculate why so much weighting should be devoted to theory work when so little time was given to it below the fourth year and in non-examination PE in the fourth and fifth years. There is no doubt that there is a great deal of knowledge in PE which perhaps has always been undervalued but was worthy of inclusion in a course in which pupils were interested. However, there appears to be no doubt that PE teachers did not want to lose practical time from normal PE periods and it was assumed that neither would pupils. It is interesting to note that now some of this knowledge is part of the National Curriculum, for example, structure and functioning of the human body and health related fitness, and knowledge of local facilities etc. As we have seen in chapter 2, in the early days of CSE, the examination boards were reluctant to accept PE as an examination subject and at first used the SSEC's statement (1963) that PE should not be examinable. They were particularly concerned with the difficulty of examining and moderating practical work. The appearance of theoretical work in the schemes did help in the introduction of PE into CSE (Carroll, 1982), and boards seemed happiest with between a 40–60 per cent split. It would appear that many teachers did follow the example of earlier schemes when submitting their own mode 3s and they were of course being advised by examining boards' moderators. Mode 3s set a precedent in the balance of theory–practical which was carried on in mode 1s. Because of the take-up, it appeared that this is what teachers wanted. When it came to GCSE this balance was accepted and there was no evidence that it was ever questioned. Syllabuses devoting 100 per cent to theoretical work have been developed since for use with mature students in sixth form and further education colleges following academic traditions.

All examining groups seem to be agreed that four or five practical activities are the ideal, and have been categorised into groups so that a balance can be achieved (table 18). They seem to agree that these should be weighted between 10 per cent and 15 per cent each. It would appear that a GCSE of less than four activities would perhaps be too specialized and not worthy of the name 'physical education', and above that, there would not be enough time to cover all the activities adequately and would be too demanding. However, the inclusion of five activities spread over three groups of major team games (for example, soccer, netball), racket sports, and individual body management type (athletics, swimming, dance, gymnastics) is very demanding in a range of abilities which have little in common. If one takes into account the theoretical cognitive demands, surely no subject demands more in terms of a spread of abilities being assessed. The problem with such a wide range of demands is that it can lead to better candidates aggregating towards the mean. There is a strong case for reducing the width of those demands by either reducing the different type of activities and/or reducing the demands on the theoretical side. This might mean a syllabus which puts more emphasis on the practical side, including putting more emphasis on diagnosis and evaluation, as in the National Curriculum, and possibly practical roles other than performer (referee and coach as in National Curriculum). In this type of syllabus too, much of the knowledge about rules, techniques, tactics, fitness and training could well be assessed in the practical situation, or perhaps with the use of video. The problem with this is that it would put more emphasis on course work, which is against the Government's policy with the recent pronouncement on the reduction of coursework in the GCSE. However, it could be that a case could be made out for practical subjects to be treated differently as it has been in the National Curriculum. There may be room for half courses too.

However, I am not advocating that all syllabuses should go along the same path. Just as it has been seen necessary to provide one-year courses for sixth forms which are all theoretical, as in the MEG Sport Studies, it would be appropriate to continue with syllabuses with the present balance. At the present time the ones on offer are too similar in content and balance, and it would be an advantage if there were more real alternatives — different and competing syllabuses. Perhaps the advent of the National Curriculum which will enforce change in the GCSE syllabuses (see chapter 8) could be regarded as an opportunity for the examining boards to get together and produce different syllabuses — one that is more practical, one more (or wholly) theoretical, one with different assessment techniques, such as projects.

Doing a Project

The NEA personal study is possibly the most controversial component in the GCSE syllabuses. Many PE teachers are against the inclusion of a project. Possibly this is because the project had gained a bad reputation in the CSE mode 3 schemes through lack of experience, supervision and control. It can be difficult to supervise a lot of different projects, and it is time consuming. However, many PE teachers, at least initially, saw the personal study as something which was done wholly in the pupils' own time and did not build it into the timetable. This is certainly a mistake, and it must be built into the course. The amount of guidance and assistance from the teacher and other people which the pupils can legitimately have is always a difficult problem, but pupils' needs will differ and in the end it is a matter of professional judgment. The value of this type of activity can easily outweigh the disadvantages. Although many pupils who are poor performers academically do badly in the personal study, there are many forms of personal study and data collection. There are many practically based studies in which an interested pupil, although not academically gifted, may do well. The NEA syllabus does encourage this: —

> A candidate may submit a personal study which includes a substantial element of practical involvement in physical activities. The work completed in the demonstration of development of skills, techniques and performances would be viewed as a method of data collection and as such research. Analysis and evaluation of this practical involvement should be included under the appropriate heading. (NEA, 1992, syllabus, p. 17)

A list of suggestions are included in the NEA scheme.

Moderation

There has often been confusion about the purpose of moderation amongst teachers new to examining. The chief examiner is responsible for the question papers in the final examination, whilst the chief moderator is responsible for practical coursework and, in the case of the NEA, the study. The chief moderator holds standardization meetings for moderators so that they will all apply the criteria in the same way. Moderators are practising teachers, and each moderator has a few schools in an area, and they arrange to visit the school to see a sample of the work. This is not the same as a final examination where all candidates would of necessity have to be seen in all activities. As a moderation may only last half a day, only a limited number of activities and a limited number of candidates can be seen. So on one visit a moderator may ask to see a sample consisting of the top performers, a group in the middle and the lowest marked performers in say, football, netball, gymnastics, trampolining and badminton which would cover the different groupings but not necessarily all activities undertaken at the school. The moderator marks the sample of candidates and the teacher is asked to do the same. A comparison is made between the moderator's marks and teacher's marks on that day to see whether the teacher is applying the criteria appropriately. The moderator will possibly ask for certain practices to be set up in order to see particular techniques or skills, or particular combinations of candidates, as well as full game or performance. It is in fact a check on the teacher's marking rather than marking the pupil. A general discrepancy in the marking of all the pupils or a particular part of the range between moderator and teacher indicates a need to adjust the teacher's marks for the particular group. This could be up or down of course. Teachers are often worried that pupils underperform on moderation day, but in theory and from a technical point of view this does not matter, as both teacher and moderator only mark what they see on that particular day. However, in practice, if they underperform it does matter to the pupil and teacher, because the pupil feels that he/she has not been able to show what they really can do and has not done justice to him/herself. The teacher, particularly new to the examination scene, often sees the pupil's performance as a reflection of his/her teaching and standards (the accountability purpose — and results are used in this way as we have seen), and low performances can give the wrong impression. It is clear that it is useful to find time for practising the activities and prepare the pupils for the moderation, particularly in activities which have not been covered for some time on the course. It would be better for moderation to take place at the end of the module when it has just been taught, particularly with the seasonal nature of most of the activities, but this is not practically or financially possible.

This model of moderation does assume that the teacher marks consistently across the range of activities not seen by the moderator. Of course a moderator will endeavour, maybe insist, that activities not seen in one year will be seen in the next. However, it is possible that a teacher does not apply the criteria consistently across activities either due to lack of experience, or lack of expertise. In the case of different teachers marking activities, difficulties can be partially overcome by standardization within the centre. My experience of standardization meetings and INSET courses suggest that those teachers with a lot of expertise in a specific activity and who have been used to working at a high level can be harsh at GCSE marking in that particular activity, and those teachers with little expertise in a given activity may not be fully conversant with the detailed criteria and may mark too leniently particularly at the low end of the scale. One may argue that those with little expertise in a given activity should not be assessing it at this level, but in a practical situation, in small schools with few staff, staff leaving or unavailable etc., staff can be forced to teach some activities they would not choose to teach, so the situation can occur. The answer is of course INSET and an attempt to gain the expertise and experience. In my experience PE teachers are good at applying the criteria in activities they have some expertise in and it is just a question of experience of applying the marks scheme. I would hazard a guess that inter-mark reliability between teachers would be very high, and there is no doubt the application of marks improves with practice.

The main problem from the examining group's point of view is the sheer number of moderators that are needed to cover all the centres and the cost of employing so many. The first problem is a technical one, the standardization of moderators. If each moderator has only half-a-dozen centres and working teachers will have a limit of around that number then with the increase in the number of centres, the number of moderators required is so large that it could be just as easy to standardize the teachers themselves. This is what the SEG have done and rely on teachers' own marking. The present system of one-day non-compulsory standardization meetings in some regions appears to be inadequate to cover all the activities. In my opinion what is required is compulsory attendance and more time spent on each activity, at least one day on each. In this way teachers could be accredited to assess specific activities in the same way as coaching or officiating, and moderators would only have need to make random checks. Moderators too could specialize and be accredited in certain activities so they would not have to cover such a wide range of activities, which at present sometimes includes activities they are not too familiar with. The accreditation of teachers to assess their own pupils will be more satisfactory than the present system. The question remains, who would do this? I suggest it could be organized by the examining boards in conjunction with the governing bodies of sports in activities where they exist, or the PEA where they do not exist, but the accreditation would be given by the examining groups themselves. The alternative is for the examining groups to do this by themselves, but the link with the governing bodies and the PEA would be valuable. There is already more cooperation between the governing bodies and the PE profession than there used to be and they have already contributed to the GCSE with their curriculum packs in specific activities, for example tennis and basketball sponsored by the Royal Navy.

Differentiation and Grading

The amalgamation of the CSE and the GCE into the GCSE brought a greater ability range into the one examination system. This was to be coped with through the process of differentiation and a new grading structure. Standards were to be maintained by the equivalence of grades — GCE standard was to set the standards in the new GCSE as it had in the previous equivalence of CSE mode 1 to a GCSE 'C' or above (see table 19). This is complicated by the change from the norm referenced (GCE, CSE) to a criterion-referencing (GCSE) system. Grade 4 CSE was the equivalent of the performance of an average ability pupil who had

Table 19: Relationship of CSE, GCE, and GCSE grades to National Curriculum levels

Before 1988 GCE	CSE	From 1988 GCSE	From 1994 NC
A		A	10
			9
B		B	8
C	1	C	7
	2		
		D	
	3		6
		E	
	4		
		F	5
	5	G	4
			3
	6		
		U	2
			1

applied him/herself to the course, so there were plenty of grade 4 or 5 and below in schools, and even if overall standards did improve, the number of lower graded pupils remained approximately the same. Moving to a seven-point grading structure and equivalence of standards in the GCSE created a greater discrimination at the top end and above the equivalent of average in the scale than the lower grades. Using the concept of differentiation the criterion measures in GCSE will still show a substantial number of pupils around the F and G, therefore just above 'ungraded'. This equivalence of standards does have a distinct bearing on the drawing up of criteria for differentiation and grade criteria and boundaries. Underlying the notion of differentiation and the criterion system is a notion of norm referencing. The old system dies hard.

There had not been a GCE in PE (though there had been one in dance) but there had been CSE Mode 1s in some regions to set the standards. The boards had to give grade descriptions for grades C and F only, though the SEG provided more than this (see the different syllabuses for descriptions). The grade descriptions are more flexible than in many other subjects such as history (see Roy, 1986) and perhaps not much use in saying what a grade C or F actually mean. The problem is that a given grade is the aggregation of a range of knowledge, skills and competences in different contexts so that it is simply not possible to state exactly

Table 20: *Effectiveness in relation to volleyball (MEG GCSE)*

Level	Description	Marks
5	Inability to dig with any degree of accuracy or to volley showing any controll.	0–3
4	Ability to demonstrate the dig and volley without an ability to establish a three-touch rally in any sequence.	4–8
3	Ability to play a three-touch rally though not in a dig, set spike order. Having knowledge of an underarm serve. Knowledge of rotation and scoring in a 6 v 6 game.	9–18
2	Ability to dig, and volley soundly and to serve underarm with consistency. Having knowledge of the spike and when to use it, of rotation and how to score in a 6 v 6 game. Show an understanding of setting from 3 and of three-touch (dig, set, spike) volleyball.	19–24
1	Ability to dig, volley, spike and serve competently in a match situation. Ability to demonstrate an overarm service, have full knowledge of rotation and how to score in a 6 v 6 game. Have an understanding of setting from 3 + 2 and of 6 cover. Ability to use any skill as required and provide evidence of the use of a basic dive.	25–35

what the different compositions of a grade are. It is not possible to detail precisely what a grade represents. Detailed grade related criteria have proved unworkable (see Kingdon and Stobart, 1987; Gipps, 1990). Grade descriptions are not likely to prove useful to say what a pupil understands, knows and can do. Of much more use is a detailed marks scheme for teachers in coursework, such as MEG's effectiveness in practical activities (example given in table 20) and NEA's personal study (see NEA, 1992 syllabus, pp. 19–20). Pupils, and parents, often want to know marks and grades but rarely know the criteria which are applied, and they often assume how well they have done just from the mark. It would be more useful for the pupils to have the criteria and to provide information of how well they are doing on that criteria. This type of information would be useful for younger pupils in formative assessment and to record their progress. Detailed criteria is too difficult to apply directly to grades because of the aggregation problem and final grades awarded lose a lot of useful information for teaching and formative assessment. The awarding of grades is a delicate one and not the simple task of applying grade to criteria because of the complexity of the criteria (see Selkirk, 1988, for discussion of the difficulties).

Differentiation is achieved through outcome and task difficulty. The idea is for all pupils of all abilities within the range to show what they 'know and can do' — a concept of positive achievement which is also at the heart of ROA. Of course, like any examination used for selection purposes, it has to differentiate pupils adequately, for use by employers and further education institutions. This concept involves both stretching the best candidates as well as not overwhelming the weakest candidates with tasks too difficult for them. This is achieved in most subjects through graded questions or differentiated papers and we have already examined the different types of questions to get at levels of knowledge and understanding in chapter 5. In the PE examination papers most of the examining groups choose grading of question difficulty, and a good example of this is in

Table 21: Entries for 'A' level PE and sport studies (numbers from the AEB and Francis, 1992)

Year	PE		Sport Studies	
	Centres	Candidates	Centres	Candidates
1988	3	34	24	232
1990	17	224	62	415
1992	112	1400	100	1200

the NEA, where there is an incline of difficulty in subsections in section A of the paper and open-ended questions in section B. The SEG and NISEAC are the only groups which offer a differentiated paper with an extended paper model, and only candidates taking this paper can get grades A and B (for details of other models of differentiation see Gipps, 1990). It can be noted that in this model (see table 17) that the percentage marks have been adjusted on the first papers. There can be grading difficulties with differentiated papers, which I will not go into here, but for the interested reader they are discussed in Selkirk (1988). In adopting a differentiated paper (the extended paper based on open-ended questions) and restricted grades, the SEG and NISEAC have put the emphasis on cognitive skills. This seems to me to be unsatisfactory in what essentially and traditionally has been a practically-based skills subject. No examining group has suggested that top grades can only be awarded to candidates who reach a certain level in practical assessment, and there would seem to me to be a stronger argument for doing so.

In practical work, differentiation is achieved through outcome. However, PE teachers do present some degree of task difficulty when they provide simple and perhaps simulated situations, for example, reduced numbers, small sided games, techniques and skills without opposition, weak opposition (see chapter 4). They also do it through less complex situations, changing the strength of team and opposition. It is expected that stronger performers will produce good technique and skills, and a wider variety of skills etc., in more complex and difficult situations than the weaker performers. As we saw in chapter 4 it is often difficult to provide the most demanding situations for the best performers if there are not enough of them. There is not the same problem in activities like gymnastics and trampolining as the best performers can be asked to produce the most difficult moves and routines.

'A' Level PE and Sport Studies

Francis (1988, 1990 and 1992) has outlined the development of 'A' levels in PE and sport studies. Table 21 shows the rapid development of interest in these two 'A' levels. The low numbers of centres and candidates in the first three years is due to the fact that they were restricted by the AEB as pilot schemes. On their approval by the SEAC in 1990 they were made available to all schools and colleges. It is anticipated that the growth will continue. According to Francis (1992) 'there are approximately 50 per cent more males than females who enter the examination' in both PE and Sport Studies, but like the GCSE, the reason for this is not apparent. It could be something to do with male and female PE teachers' attitudes to the examination, or male and female students' attitudes to PE.

Both syllabuses have a lot in common. Their approach is a higher education one, with a core and option programme based on the disciplines of anatomy and physiology, biomechanics, psychology, sociology and history. The main difference is that Sport Studies includes a research-based project (20 per cent) whilst PE includes a practical performance component (30 per cent). In effect, the 30 per cent practical assessment is not totally devoted to practical performance because almost half of it goes in observation and analysis of performance. This is in line with the thinking in the National Curriculum and in future it is likely that candidates will have much greater experience of this aspect than they do at present. The predominance of theoretical work and cognitive type assessment is understandable at 'A' level, where it fits in with the 'A' level ethos, and prepares students for higher education.

Some of the difficulties in teaching the 'A' level syllabuses have been raised by Carroll (1990a), Alderson (1988) and Wilmut (1988). In both the syllabuses the strong discipline structure fragments the course and affects course cohesion, and the twin demands of breadth in terms of the range of disciplines and depth within each discipline are rarely demanded in one syllabus at this level. The additional demand of the research project or practical performance makes it difficult for candidates to achieve the highest grades (see Francis, 1992).

On analyzing the demands of the question papers, it would appear that Sports Studies makes greater demands in terms of the type of questions. There are more essay-type questions in Sport Studies whilst more structured, shorter answers are required in PE. The project is also demanding, and the criteria for marking suggests that the classical experimental design finds most favour, and may prove limiting. There are clearly many ways to carry out an investigation and methods of presentation and there should be more flexibility to give credit for what students can do. The practical component in PE is not without criticism either. The assessment of two activities out of a total of only seven activities divided into two groups is also restrictive. The two groupings are:

(i) basketball, badminton, hockey, tennis;
(ii) athletics, gymnastics, swimming.

Noticeable absentees are soccer and netball amongst others. These absentee activities include some of the central activities in a secondary school curriculum, activities which have been performed and studied for many years including GCSE. The restriction may even be regarded as sexist depending on previous schooling. Although it would clearly be difficult for 'A' level teachers to cope with a large number of activities and inevitably there will always be some restriction placed by the teachers themselves, this list needs to be looked at if credibility is to be maintained and candidates allowed to show what they can do. The so-called physical preparation section has been criticized in chapter 3 as an inappropriate use of a fitness type test.

In the physical performance section marks are given for techniques, skills and overall performance but there is an attempt to standardize the marking by relating the performance to a representative standard of play, national, regional, county, schools etc. The problem with this is that the representative criteria is variable. School, club, county and regional levels vary enormously depending upon where one lives, and the opportunities which exist to actually become representative will also vary enormously depending on the activity and the year. Although it does not state the candidate actually has to represent the particular level, the standards operating in the school/college area will be the ones used. Although the attempt to standardize is laudable, this aspect needs to be looked at. The tying of marks so closely with representation could cause problems, schools will find it difficult to have many pupils of regional (for example, northwest, southern standards) or even county standards. Also it would be difficult for a moderator to revise marks if pupils had been selected at any of these levels when they had come from an area or year when the standards were low (compare say county standards of a small or a sparsely populated county with Lancashire or Surrey). The issues of moderation discussed under GCSE above apply also to 'A' level PE.

Francis (1992) has indicated that initially there had been a problem about the acceptability of 'A' level PE and Sport Studies for university entrance, but once this came out of the pilot stage and had been approved by the SEAC, universities and higher education institutions accepted them on a par with other 'A' levels. A student was accepted at the University of Oxford on the basis of three 'A' levels one of which was PE (Francis, 1990).

Getting Started in an Examination Scheme

It may be the case that the PE teacher has to convince the headteacher or other authorities of the value and need to have a GCSE course in PE. This may be because they see the PE role in a different way to many PE teachers, but it may be also because they can make savings on staff and resources. Therefore a strong case may have to be made out for the proposal, which needs to have a careful and logical rationale to show the benefits for pupils and the school, the resources needed and organization of the course. The headteacher is more likely to be impressed with a well-reasoned case with issues and problems aired than a mere request for GCSE PE. It would also be helpful if the PE department could put on a united front to support the case. In the past, development has been hampered by division within the department, between male and female colleagues, and the full expertise of the department has not been available for use on a course.

Probably the first choice a teacher has to make is to decide which syllabus to undertake. In the GCSE there has been a strong regional bias, left over from the CSE days and in the beginning some local authorities or schools recommended their regional board very strongly. A teacher should select the syllabus based on what suits staff and the pupils best. However, some teachers select a syllabus before considering all the implications. They need to look at the content, assessment procedures and differences between them in relation to their staff expertise, school facilities, resources and their ability to deliver. Some teachers did embark on schemes without considering all these details and met some problems. A comparison on some of these aspects has been shown in tables 17 and 18. It is a good idea to consult staff in other schools who have experience of examination work. After selecting the syllabus, it is important to make a detailed plan for the whole of the first and second years course. This means detailing the number of lessons each term which will be spent on the different parts of the scheme, both practical and theory, and who will teach them. Summer term examination dates for moderation and deadlines for coursework must be taken into consideration in the planning. I have been surprised at the large number of teachers coming on INSET programmes who have not done this exercise. They have a 'rough' idea of when they will teach topics or activities, some even just start to teach the theory part. It is very easy to get the timing wrong and spend far too long on a section of the syllabus which does not warrant it. An analysis of the question papers and mark schemes will give a guide to how long to spend on a section of the syllabus. This gives a guide to the depth of teaching required which is often a great concern to teachers new to the syllabus.

If one is following a syllabus in which there is a project, as in NEA GCSE, and 'A' level sport studies, time for consultation and tutoring and possibly marking the project must be built in. With the GCSE it should certainly be given curriculum timetable space. Many PE teachers made the error of omitting the study from their timetable, thinking it was to be entirely done in the candidates' own time, and the result was that pupils suffered from lack of advice and handed in weaker studies than they would have done. Pupils do need guidance in choice of topics, methods of collecting data, or whatever it is they are doing, and should be aware of the criteria for marking. For the theory section there has been a shortage of resources. Beashell and Taylor's two books (1986 and 1988) have filled this gap to a certain extent, but time to plan coursework assignments and to collect other material from other sources, such as local facilities, Sports Council, news and other books can be seriously underestimated by inexperienced teachers.

On the practical side, the activities, facilities and staff have all got to be co-ordinated, and this is probably something the PE teacher will already understand. However, the following do need to be considered:

Will a choice of activities be allowed?

Will more activities be taught and the best performances only count in the assessment?

Has enough time been allowed for assessment and to show what each can do?

Will there be specific time put aside for assessment or can it take place in normal teaching?

In some syllabuses a pupil is allowed to be assessed in activities not necessarily undertaken in the school as long as it can be moderated. However, the teacher is responsible for the assessment. So what arrangements have been made for verifying claims made by pupils and for assessing performance?

Some examining groups allow a school to submit a syllabus in a practical activity not on their list. If a teacher decides to do this, it is advisable to put it in the same format as the published activities and to meet the regulations and procedures precisely, otherwise it will be turned down. It is essential to make sure

Table 22: Number of BTEC registrations by level and gender for leisure studies

Level	1987–88			1989–90				1991–92			
	M	F	Total	M	F	NK	Total	M	F	NK	Total
First	759	239	998	553	536	5	1094	1295	833	16	2144
National	789	580	1369	1572	969	1	2542	3059	1626	55	4740
Higher National	69	81	150	136	111	0	247	582	397	1	980
TOTAL	1617	900	2517	2261	1616	6	3883	4936	2856	72	7864

Table 23: Number of BTEC awards by level and gender for leisure studies

Level	1991/92			
	M	F	NK	Total
First	873	656	10	1539
National	1363	940	0	2303
Higher National	132	136	0	268
TOTAL	2368	1732	10	4110

the activity has been approved before allowing a pupil to believe he/she will be assessed in it.

The success of a new course can depend on the intake of students on that course. It is important to get a full range of the ability levels, particularly now with the emphasis placed on results, and in some schools this has not always been the case in PE. Therefore a careful look at the examination subject group options and combinations is required, and the PE teacher may have to argue a case for the groupings and combinations which gives the best chance for the full ability range.

The challenge, value and meeting the problems of establishing the new courses has been indicated by teachers in the field, for example, Murphy (1990) in relation to the GCSE, Nicholas (1990) for 'A' level PE, and Marsden (1990) for Sport Studies 'A' level.

Vocational Schemes

In recent years there has been a considerable growth in vocational qualifications in the recreational and leisure industry. As sport is part of this industry, and because of the close link between sport and PE, teachers and lecturers in PE have changed direction and oriented towards teaching these vocational qualifications, especially in further education and sixth-form colleges (see table 4). Indeed it was usually PE staff in colleges who took the lead in developing these courses. Thus the 1980s saw the introduction and development of the Certificate of Pre-Vocational Education (CPVE), City and Guilds of London Institute (C&G) 781 syllabus, and Business and Technology Education Council (BTEC) validated courses in recreation and leisure. One of the features of the early years has been a very rapid expansion in the number of centres and candidates for all these courses, illustrated by the BTEC figures in tables 22 and 23. This expansion is continuing and the range of courses has broadened, for example, BTEC has over 300 students registered on sport science courses. There has also been a rapid growth of degree course in the higher education sector. One might suggest that it is a phenomenal expansion, and in spite of the growth of the industry in many areas of activities, one might also wonder whether all the students will find employment within the industry especially if the recession continues. What is noticeable from both the C&G and BTEC figures is the dominance of males and these figures suggest that there are more qualified men than women going into the recreational and leisure industries.

CPVE, C&G and BTEC have different structures. CPVE was developed for post-16 for those not going on to academic courses. Inevitably it suffered from low status problems. It offers core units of general use in many educational institutions and in employment, such as communication skills. Colleges have developed specialized units many of which have been developed in relation to recreation, leisure and physical education. Assessment is carried out internally. BTEC has a similar structure with its core programmes applicable to many industries and core and optional units in the leisure industry. BTEC offers four levels roughly equivalent to types of employment as follows;

First, National, Higher National and Continuing Education;

Initial, Technician, Supervisory and Management.

C&G opts for a four-part structure, Marketing, Provision and Control, Resource Management and Product Knowledge. C&G is geared more to sport and recreation through its product knowledge section. Like BTEC it has a four-level structure. The difference between C&G and BTEC is that C&G is an examining body and produces a syllabus, whilst BTEC is a validating body and syllabuses are developed by individual institutions. Both C&G and BTEC have four-part structures, but these levels are not directly equivalent. At the lower levels C&G appears to be more practical and competency-based, whilst BTEC courses often have more academic content.

At the time of writing all vocational courses for all industries are in the process of change. This has been brought about by the establishment of the National Council for Vocational Qualifications (NCVQ). Scotland has its own council, the Scottish Council for Vocational Education (SCOTVEC). Now all courses and qualifications have to have the NCVQ seal of approval. This has been done through the NCVQ setting up Industry Lead Bodies (ILB) for each industry which outlines the competencies required and sets the standards for that industry. In this way, the needs of the industry will be met, everyone will know the competencies required for a particular job and the levels demanded, and there will be parity across qualifications.

It was clear then that the City and Guilds and BTEC courses would have to be changed and directed to more job specific competencies and give more on the job training in order to get accreditation. However it has been difficult for institutions to provide this part of the training for full-time students, thus General National Vocational Qualifications (GNVQ) have been introduced and have been piloted at levels 2 and 3 from September 1992. GNVQ 2 is the equivalent of BTEC first or four GCSEs, whilst GNVQ is similar to a BTEC National Diploma or two 'A' levels. Although this will meet the institutions' problem, it may only serve to confuse the industry in the early days.

Within the recreation and leisure industries, lead bodies were set up in different sectors, such as sport and recreation and health and fitness. To go into all of the areas would not be appropriate here, but to show what has been happening, I will briefly outline the structure of sport and recreation. The ILB for Sport and Recreation consisted of a Chairman from: the Sports Council; Vice-chairman and secretariat; employer representation from: the voluntary sector (two), the private sector (two), the public sector (three); employer representation from four different unions; advisers from the NCVQ, the Training Agency, SCOTVEC and ILAM; and representatives from research consultancies (three) and a project coordinator. The ILB commissioned research to identify the skills, knowledge and qualities needed in the industry and identified six occupational areas. These are:

   Coaching, teaching and instructing
   Facility management
   Operational services
   Outdoor education
   Play and playwork
   Sports development

The ILB established Technical Standards Working Groups (TSWGs) for each area which will identify job competencies standards and development.

Recreation v. Vocation

Academic v. Vocation

There has been a complete change of direction in PE departments in colleges of further education, from recreational PE to vocational training (see table 4), which has brought them in line with the rest of the college. This meant that most PE teachers who had been traditionally trained were ill-equipped for this change. Although they had specific knowledge of sports and coaching they lacked the knowledge required for the leisure courses and most had no relevant experience of the industry unlike their colleagues in other departments. These teachers had to acquire this professional development, and many have had to make close links with the industry. This has been possible at the lower levels of C&G and BTEC, but their lack of experience in the industry has been a drawback with the development of NVQs. In future most of the posts in FE colleges teaching these types of courses will require staff who have some experience of the leisure industry. This gives them more credibility. Movement from schools to FE colleges of PE staff without the appropriate experience or qualifications of the industry is now likely to be limited in spite of the development of GNVQs.

A recent government white paper has replaced CPVE with a 14–19 age range programme at three levels. The first is the foundation. This would allow PE teachers to come in and offer foundation courses which could be related to the sport and recreation industry. Because of what I have said above about the teachers' likely lack of knowledge in the wider fields of recreation and leisure, teachers could concentrate on aspects related to coaching, officiating, administration of sport, community provision and health and fitness. This would also be in line with development in the National Curriculum, though of course, some of the aspects would be taken further than the National Curriculum and could be given a vocational orientation.

However, what appears to prevent the development of foundation courses for vocational qualifications is the introduction of the National Curriculum itself and the status given to vocational qualifications in education. With the development of NVQs and GNVQs led by industry itself there should be no question of the status of vocational qualifications by employers. However, in schools it is different. The whole thrust of education appears to be related to more academic type qualifications, GCSEs and 'A' levels and the prestigious route to higher education in spite of the fact that a proportion of the school population does not appear suited to this type of education. The National Curriculum has reemphasized the importance of the academic subjects, although the inclusion of technology may be seen as a gesture to some application of theory. The problem also appears to be that the amount of time required to carry out the core and foundation subjects has not left enough time for development of cross-curricular and vocational courses.

The government has indicated its intention of valuing and supporting vocational training, and the importance placed on education and training in relation to industry is suggested by the Technical and Vocational Educational Initiative (TVEI), the establishment of the NCVQ and NVQs, and TECs (Technical and Education Council). However, they have developed all of these initiatives separately. So the National Curriculum was developed without reference to educational and vocational qualifications as a whole. The GCSE is to be the main means of assessing Key Stage 4, but the opportunity was missed to consider its relation to 'A' levels and vocational qualifications. Thus the 'A' level and sixth form qualifications debate continues. It is well known that many continental countries have developed a dual system of academic and vocational qualifications where both are equally valued within the schooling system. The Government failed to look at this possibility in its haste to introduce the National Curriculum. However, because of greater links with EC countries and the constant search for higher standards and comparability with our European neighbours, they may be forced to rethink on the National Curriculum and vocational qualifications. It would certainly be possible for PE teachers, for instance, to offer recreation and sport courses which could be accredited as modules or units by both GCSE examining groups and by NVQ as GNVQs. There is already a travel and tourism GCSE which bridges this gap of the academic-vocational divide.

Governing Body Award Schemes

This chapter cannot be completed without brief mention being made of the governing body award schemes. After all they have been around longer than examinations in PE.

It is difficult to find out exactly how many schemes there are, how many children undertake them and the use made of them in the schools. In a survey of

160 organizations, Kelly (1986) received ninety-five replies and identified sixty separate award schemes for the 8–14 age group. Since that date it is known that other schemes have been developed, for example, the Lawn Tennis scheme. Kelly also reported that thirty-seven of the award schemes had no specified aims in the literature, twenty-two of the schemes did not require the assessor or tester to hold any qualifications in the activity, and sponsors are quoted on twenty-four schemes. Kelly makes the important points of the need for clear aims and to set standards. There does appear to be a wide disparity between assessors which is inevitable if there are no minimum qualifications for assessors and no guidance for assessment. The award schemes no doubt need the sponsors but the use of education as a cheap form of advertising is dubious. Kelly also surveyed primary and secondary schools in two local authorities to find out the use made of award schemes. The most popular schemes in the primary schools were swimming, gymnastics, athletics, football, and in secondary schools, gymnastics, swimming, cross country running, athletics, badminton, basketball and hockey. There were slight differences between the two authorities and especially in the provision for swimming. Schemes were more likely to be offered in the secondary sector than the primary, and, on average, four schemes were offered in each secondary to two per primary school.

What is more important than the quantity of schemes and their availability in schools is the use made of them by the teachers. Unfortunately this is something not brought out fully by Kelly. It is not certain how these schemes fit in with the teachers' schemes of work. It is clear from my discussion with teachers over the years and from Kelly's interviews that they are used as a motivating force. It is quite common for teachers to say, 'children like to wear badges', and 'It is a sense of achievement', and statements like these can be found in Kelly's interviews with teachers (*ibid*). However, this motivational element and sense of achievement can have its worrying side when teachers say,

> Well I think as far as the children are concerned, primarily, who's best in class, then the ones who are best in class — are they best in the year? (Interview with teacher, *ibid*)

What concerns me about this is the emphasis on comparability with other children (norm reference), the competition and ego orientation, as opposed to the self-referencing, skill and learning orientation which the awards could foster. I am referring here to the climate which the teacher encourages and provides and the use made of these awards within that climate. Everyone cannot be best in the class or year and self-referencing and individual sense of achievement may be more motivating for more children in the long run. As indicated in chapter 4, I am not so naive as to think that children will not compare themselves, but the use made of these awards is important. It can feature as an important part of ROA. However, the overemphasis of testing, the time consuming nature of some of the testing and the neglect of teaching can mitigate against the use of these awards and be demotivating. It is essential that they are used judiciously, fit into the schools' schemes of work, and used in an appropriate educational climate. Otherwise we might find that appearances and display, testing and certificates are more important than the physical education of the child, and the sponsors will gain more from the schemes than the children.

Chapter 7

Recording Achievement

Are ROA Achieving Their Purposes?

Although events moved quickly in the 1980s in respect of Government action and implementation of policies in respect of ROA, the ideas and purposes of records were not new and one could suggest it had taken the government forty years to react to the Norwood Report (Board of Education, 1943). PE teachers will find it interesting to note that games were specifically mentioned.

> The first part would contain a record of the share which the pupil had taken in the general life of the school, games, societies and the like. It would, in short, give the reader some idea of the way in which he had used the opportunities offered to him by his education, using the term in its widest sense. (p. 48)

The second part referred inevitably to examination results. The main concern here (and since) was the unsatisfactory nature of examination certificates as a school leaving document and a record of pupils' achievements. Many pupils were leaving without any certification at all or with a minimum of examination entries/passes. The aim then was primarily a summary document, as were many of the early attempts at ROA, for example the Record of Personal Achievement (RPA) in Swindon from 1969 (Swales, 1979), the Evesham High School Personal Achievement Record (PAR) in 1979, the Scottish Council for Research in Education (SCRE) profile in 1976 (SCRE, 1977). These developments saw the introduction of pupil recording, and the inclusion of personal qualities and achievements in non-academic subjects.

PE is, of course, regarded as non-academic and is strong in personal qualities, and achievements in PE are something which many pupils will value. However, these early attempts did have the stigma of a 'low ability image' and credibility in some quarters as a leaving document. There were still only a small number of schools involved in ROA by 1980 (twenty-five according to Balogh, 1982), but despite the low status image and difficulties, their value to all pupils was being considered. The early 1980s saw developments in Wiltshire and through a liaison of four local authorities with the University of Oxford Delegacy of Local Examinations (OCEA) in 1982 (Fairbairn, 1988), which were the beginnings of accreditation and validation by outside bodies to give credibility and value to the development. So when the DES took up ROA as policy (DES, 1984), and the Government funded pilot schemes, it was taking up a 'grass roots' development, furthering and resourcing an educational and socio-political need. However, the original purposes had widened since the early days to become a document for all pupils. The purposes outlined in 1984 were reiterated in an evaluation report (PRAISE) (DES, 1988) and the Records of Achievement National Steering Committee (RANSC) (DES, 1989a). They were stated as follows, with my classification in brackets.

(i) Recognition of achievement. Records and recording systems should recognize, acknowledge and give credit for what pupils have achieved and experienced, not just in terms of public examinations but in other ways as well. They should do justice to pupils' own efforts and to the efforts of the teachers, parents, ratepayers and taxpayers to give them a good education. (Summative Recognition, Accountability).

(ii) Motivation and Personal Development. They should contribute to pupils' personal development and progress by improving their motivation, providing encouragement and increasing their awareness of strengths, weaknesses and opportunities. (Formative, Feedback, Diagnostic, Motivation).

(iii) Curriculum and Organization. The recording process should help schools to identify the all-round potential of their pupils and to consider how well their curriculum, teaching and organisation enable pupils to develop the general, practical and social skills which are to be recorded. (Identify potential, Teacher evaluation of curriculum and practice, Development of pupils, Formative)

(iv) A Document of Record . . . a short summary document of record which is recognized and valued by employers and institutions of further and higher education. To help users decide how pupils could be best employed or further training. (Summative, Certification, Selection outside the school). (DES, 1989a, p. 5)

So it has to be 'all things to all men', or rather, 'all things to all pupils and teachers'. The Government expects it to serve a multiplicity of purposes, some of which may be, if not in conflict, at least not in harmony with each other. Hargreaves (1989) proposes:

> . . . that these two purposes, motivational and selective, are fundamentally incompatible in important respects. (p. 118)

He is, in fact, arguing that ROA cannot solve the motivational 'crisis' in schools nor the socio-political or economic 'crises' outside schools. This raises the question whether ROA can achieve its multiplicity of purposes. Are ROA being asked to do too much? This is in fact a very basic and serious issue, because a teacher must know the purposes of ROA in order to make the assessment and then to record the information. What may be of use to employers, FE or HE for selection purposes may be of no use in motivating the pupils or of use in formative assessment or in curriculum evaluation. So, whereas the employer or HE might be interested in the amount, level of interest and participation in physical activity and sports, the pupil needs to know his/her strengths and weaknesses in context of the activity and what he/she needs to do next, whilst the teacher needs to know the overall progress to see whether his/her curriculum is satisfactory. Moreover, the requirement of formative assessment with the principle of pupils' involvement in their own assessment and recording and teacher-pupil discussion (DES, 1989a), means more than merely recording achievement and experience, it means for most teachers a complete change in curricular pedagogy and styles of teaching and learning. This is particularly so in PE, where this means that teachers and schools have not only to cope with the administration and management problems of ROA, but also with changing teaching methods and philosophies. This latter is, of course, much harder to do.

Schools have responded to these demands in a variety of ways, but have basically attempted to meet these purposes by developing formative and summative documents, and whole school policies on ROA and assessment. How far any one ROA or school has achieved all these purposes is difficult to say. The report on the national evaluation of pilot schemes suggests that purposes one (recognition of achievement) and four (provision of a summary document) have been fulfilled, but the way these purposes are met 'are crucial to the fulfillment of purposes two and three' (DES, 1988, pp. 157–8). Questions still remained on what should be included, what are the boundary limits of recording, and the collection and presentation and credibility of a summary document. Whilst there is evidence of employers' interest in and use of ROA in the PRAISE report and elsewhere, for example, Mackrell in SERA Profile (1987), it is not always easy to find direct evidence of the effects of ROA. The PRAISE report points to how difficult it is to point to evidence which directly links pupils' changes in attitudes to ROA, although many teachers are very enthusiastic in reporting beneficial effects. The report does point to different types of motivation arising from the ROA, the intrinsic associated with recording and taking more responsibility for their learning, and the extrinsic related to the product of the document. Benefits in these directions, and in teacher-pupil relations, in expectations, in self-esteem, in self-awareness and reflection on own ability were all reported (DES, 1988). However, Phillips (1989) study of pupils' opinions show that students themselves identified constraints in recording, which adversely affected motivation, teacher-pupil relations and the values of ROA. Establishing the 'right' classroom climate and teacher-pupil relations appears to be the crucial message from this study.

The PRAISE report shows that there were some effects in relation to purpose three (curriculum teaching and organization), that is, ROA did have an effect on some teachers' thinking. However, it does say that:

> The picture that emerges is of a developmental continuum, at one end of which are teachers who remain relatively untouched by such new developments or who are torn by their conflicting demands. Other teachers are at various points along the continuum with some at the far end, who have succeeded in fully operationalizing a pedagogy, which has clear objectives, individual targets and offers pupils a full partnership in the learning process. (DES, 1988, pp. 162–3)

As this was very early days this should not be surprising especially if it is realized how difficult it can be to change fundamental thinking, particularly if a teacher feels a development is being imposed (see Sparkes, 1991a).

The PRAISE report does mention the blurring of the academic/pastoral boundary, and the formative/summative boundary (DES, 1988), which affects curriculum and organization. In an overall summary the report states:

> The evidence we have reported, particularly in part one of this report makes it clear that relatively few schools have as yet fully worked through the implications of this philosophy. That is to say, few as yet have fulfilled all four of the record of achievement purposes. What they have done, however, through their efforts — and this is very important — is to clarify the issues involved. Furthermore they may have provided palpable and powerful testimony that the rationale of the initiative itself is educationally sound. (p. 166)

How far do ROA in PE meet these purposes? As the PRAISE team found, it is often difficult to substantiate claims with evidence which directly shows the direct link between ROA and achievement of the purpose. An examination of the many ROA I have been able to collect and those published (for example, Booton, 1986; Hatfield and Phillips, 1989) would suggest that they do achieve the purpose of recording and recognizing achievement (purpose one) in physical skills, personal qualities and extra-curricular skills, which would do justice to pupils' efforts and be helpful to parents. How far the PE comments would be useful to employers and FE is difficult to establish. Some ROA did contain negative statements, which certainly should be avoided at the summary stage and is against the principle of recording positive achievements. Booton (1986) reported that seventy local firms were asked what they were looking for in prospective employees. The answers directly related to PE were physical fitness for the job, and manual or finger dexterity, whilst other answers which could be assessed in PE were appearance, punctuality, attendance, ability to understand instructions, capacity to work without supervision, honesty and integrity. Mackrell (1987) gives some support to the view that employers value the personal and interpersonal qualities and skills, though, at that stage, he suggested it still had to be sold to them. One would expect that employers would prefer healthy, physically active and fit individuals and ROA could show that to a certain extent by detailing participation in activities. There has been concern about childrens' lifestyles and effects on their health, particularly coronary heart disease which starts in childhood (Armstrong, 1990; ITV ch. 4, 1992). This is something that employers should be aware of and concerned about as it could cost them working days. This is a message which also probably still needs to be sold to them.

The difficulty of evaluating whether purposes two and three are being achieved has been mentioned above and by the PRAISE team (DES, 1988). Comments by many teachers suggest that pupils are motivated by ROA, but some teachers do suggest that pupils get bored and see recording as school work just like any other work which supports Phillips' comments (1989). However, a study by Jepson and Carroll (1991) who introduced ROA in PE to selected years in a school whilst others continued with reports only, asked pupils their opinions on ROA and reports. The results showed that ROA were better than reports at motivation, better at recognizing the pupils' own strengths and weaknesses, better at helping them make progress and better at showing what is important to them (all these results were statistically significant at the 1 per cent level on a chi square test). Although the authors concede that there may be effects such as the newness of ROA, teacher interest and involvement as action researcher, their work does suggest that ROA are a better system and do achieve purpose two (motivation) of the DES 1989 policy.

As for curriculum and pedagogical change (purpose three), change is indicated by the introduction of pupil assessment, target setting and pupil recording as indicated in Booton (1986), Hatfield and Phillips (1989) and Jepson and Carroll (1991). How far teachers can go along this path in view of the time management problem, the context (location) in gymnasium, swimming pools and playing fields, the threat to active learning time, and safety considerations is very difficult to say. There may be some conflict, and solutions may require delicate balancing and compromise. There is the appropriateness to the context of the activity and stage of the learner to consider as well as pure style of teaching (see Mosston, 1986, for styles). The training and philosophies of teachers are difficult to change as Sparkes (1991a) has shown in the PE context.

What Should be Recorded?

As we have seen there are different purposes and the need for both a summary document and formative documents. Consequently what is recorded in both documents will often be different though related, as the summary document will be compiled through the formative assessment documents. RANSC (DES, 1989a) gave some guidelines on content for the summary document. ROA should contain (examples, those related to PE)

Subject specific achievement	National Curriculum
	Examinations
	Others
Cross-curricular achievements such as	Careers
	Health
	PSE
General skills	Communication skills
	Coordination, dexterity
	Personal skills, reliability and enthusiasm
Extra-curricular and out-of-school activities	Work experience
	School activities, for example, sport
	Leisure interests

Principles which are relevant to the content included,
factual base record, in narrative form,
presented in context, can be authenticated,
constructive statements on achievement (not failure).

A National Record of Achievement document has been developed, interestingly by the Employment Department, formerly the Training Agency (Employment Dept, 1991). The headings consist of:

Personal details, schools attended, validation scheme
Employment history
Personal statement to record own assessment of progress, to identify potential, other information
Achievement and Experiences – this includes general skills, cross-curricular skills and extra curricular as indicated in the RANSC report above.
Qualifications and credits – externally certificated
School achievements – completion by school – each subject, National Curriculum statutory assessments, summary of performance showing level, attendance record.

These headings provide space for open comments on one side of A4 paper for each heading. They are expected to be updated on leaving school. The aim is to standardize ROA, which will give it more credibility, and provide a format which all employers and educational institutions will recognize and know. 'The ultimate aim is to produce one single system of recording achievement throughout life which both the process encompassed by the National Record of Vocational Achievement (NROVA) and the summary NRA will form a part.' (Employment Dept, 1991).

Clearly then it also has a longer term goal to be used throughout education and employment, and it remains to be seen whether this more ambitious aim can be achieved. At present there is an attempt to make the NRA acceptable to HE institutions through a research project based at Wigan, the Recording Achievement and Higher Education Project.

The RANSC report did not give any guidelines for a formative document which suggests the Government is putting greater emphasis on the summary document, but the summary document does depend on the prior development of adequate formative documents if it is to encompass such a wide range of achievements. Formative documents will, of necessity, include all the above skills and achievements but will not be hampered by the space limit (four sides of A4 in total) (DES, 1989a), or the principles mentioned above. Therefore to be useful in the formative stage, it will contain more than factual based statements — these will be evaluative, will identify strengths and weaknesses and thereby negative statements, can contain projection or targets and personal opinions.

We have already dealt with what can and should be assessed in chapter 3. The decision then is what should be recorded. Quite clearly no attempt should be made to record everything, it must be selective in order for it to be manageable and useful. There is a difficulty of separating *what* should be recorded from *how, when and who* does the recording, because it raises the issues of manageability which includes a time dimension. These issues are perhaps more acute in PE than in classroom subjects because of the location and conditions under which PE takes place, such as gymnasia and sports halls, or outside where the weather must be considered — playing fields, outdoor swimming pools and other urban or rural venues. The development of departmental and whole school policies, tutorial systems, computers, and technical assistance have helped overcome some of the

Example 1 Example 2

Hockey — Skills Achieved Tick	Very Well	Good	Satisfactory	Poor	Very Poor
I can show basic grip on the skills.					
I can receive a pass from the front (right, left).					
I can do a push pass.					
I can hit the ball while moving.					
I can do a tackle.					
i can dribble the ball.					
Other skills					

Example 3

Skill Achieved	3 or 5 Point Scale
	Technique Correct ———————————— Correction Needed
	Everytime ———————————————— Once
	Under Pressure ———————————— Demonstration

Figure 8: Showing examples of tick lists for skills achieved

problems in some schools. To overcome the time management problem, in PE it has been common to adopt a tick box format for skills/techniques to show what a pupil has achieved in a physical activity at specific times (figure 8). Sometimes this is later turned into a narrative statement.

In PE there seems little disagreement over the recording of physical skills in an activity, it is the detail and format which varies. After all, this is the heart of the subject, the achievement of physical skills is the product. What recording has done, like GCSE, has been to make PE teachers more precise over the techniques and skills required, to state them categorically, to make pupils more aware of them, to set pupils' targets and to check whether all pupils can achieve them. A list of recorded skills in a physical activity is given in figure 8 with three examples, two of which contain an evaluative judgment of the performance. This is more useful, because physical skills are rarely 'can do', 'can't do' in relation to all situations, particularly in games. Situational factors and level are important. It does raise the issue of when should a skill be recorded. When it is performed?, once?, twice?, in or out of game or competition context?, only in a full game or competitive context?, in the formative context?. The answer is likely to vary. It is an achievement to do something for the first time, even out of a full pressured context, and it may well be worth recording for that pupil, but, if it cannot be repeated or cannot be repeated in a competitive situation then it may not be much use for the future. This is where targeting comes in. A target can be set to do it again, and to repeat it under more difficult conditions, under competitive situations, to refine and improve the technique and skill usage. Situations can be set up to specifically achieve these targets. Targeting is not assessment, of course, nor does it have to be recorded, but it does relate to achievement. In PE many of the ROA do not include targets but some do. It gives something for the pupil to work towards, and then, at the end of a period of time, to evaluate whether it has been achieved. Recording the targets will always be a reminder to the pupils of their immediate goals and what they will have to assess. An example of targeting is shown in figure 9, 'What I can do to improve', from Great Sankey HS, (Hatfield and Phillips, 1989).

The National Curriculum requirements add further skills related to the planning and evaluation of performance which should be recorded as they relate to statutory end of key stages and programmes of study. This will mean altering current ROA to take these into account. The demands of the National Curriculum will be discussed under a separate heading (chapter 8).

When it comes to the recording of general and personal skills, PE teachers do not seem to have had much trouble with communication skills, coordination, which is gleaned from their physical skills, cooperation with others, and there are plenty of opportunities for all of these in PE activities. However, some of the other skills or qualities have been much more problematic. We have seen the difficulty of assessing many of the personal qualities in chapter 3. Although teachers are continually assessing pupils' behaviour and personal qualities, and clearly have to deal with pupils' behaviour which reflects characteristics and qualities, it is one thing to informally assess and deal with these, it is quite another to record them. Recording these qualities appears to make them that much more objective, more definitive, more permanent. The evidence for some of these qualities is often ephemeral and intangible, and may be context specific. These recorded qualities may well be used in selection by employers and educational institutions who deal with very different working conditions. Pupils may well exhibit very different qualities in working contexts than school contexts, and this goes for pupils who exhibit strong anti-work tendencies in school.

I have seen the following qualities amongst others recorded (for example, Booton, 1986; Hatfield and Phillips, 1989).

Hardworking
Listening to and following instructions
Behaviour standards
Appearance
Punctuality
Working independently
Cooperation with others
Asking questions
Communication
Attitude to care of equipment
Considerate to other pupils
Enthusiasm
Confidence
Work without supervision
Initiative and leadership qualities
Politeness

Achievements

(f) How well did I do in the field events?

(g) How well did I do in the track events?

(h) How well did I understand the coaching points?

(i) How much did I enjoy this unit?

How to Target

1 Poor

2 Could be better

3 Good

4 Very Good

What I can do to improve

1 ....

2 ....

Personal Qualities

(a) How hardworking am I?

(b) How good am I at listening to instructions?

(c) How good am I at following instructions?

(d) How good was my behaviour?

(f) How well did I remember my kit?

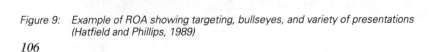

Figure 9: Example of ROA showing targeting, bullseyes, and variety of presentations (Hatfield and Phillips, 1989)

Reliability
Perception
Positive attitudes/motivation

These tend to be qualities which teachers and pupils can find evidence for, but the evidence can often be open to different interpretations. The value of teacher-pupil discussion on these points has proved valuable to either teacher or pupil but they may have to beg to differ.

Whether fitness should be recorded is open to debate. We have already seen the difficulties of assessment (Armstrong, 1987 and 1990), so recording could be open to misinterpretation, as the National Curriculum and examination results certainly have been. Nevertheless, for the future, if we could get over some of the problems, they could be a useful record for certain employment avenues where they require some form of basic fitness, such as the police and armed forces. Certainly participation in physical activities, frequency and level can be included.

The main issues surrounding extra-curricular and leisure interests and achievements are the limits of recording and authentication. Phillips (1989) and Hargreaves (1989) have commented on the confidentiality issue. Clearly there are limits to what should and can be recorded, and Hargreaves warns of judicious use of some types of activities in the interests of the child. Not many of these are likely to fall into the PE teacher's realm, except possibly as a more general tutor, but something like taking part in a conservation protest, thought to be worthy of comment by some teachers, may be construed as 'activist' or 'troublemaker' by some readers and users of the ROA. Some teachers feel they do need to authenticate outside school achievements as indicated by the RANSC report (DES, 1989a), but others feel this shows distrust.

How Should ROA be Presented?

There are many ways in which the record can be presented. PE teachers may find there is a school format which they have to fit into. Some schools have given departments leeway to provide their own format in formative documents. This has allowed PE teachers to use variations, for example, Trinity HS, Manchester, incorporates their PE ROA in a booklet which also contains information, quizzes, interesting facts, and gives a certificate at the end of the year. This type of presentation, along with others such as the use of cartoons, make it interesting or amusing, and is clearly done to keep the pupils' interest and motivation. Most ROA appear more straightforward, workmanlike and serious documents. Some of the main forms used are:

(a)   Tick lists of achievements
Figure 8 shows three examples of this format. There is usually a list for each activity and is normally completed by the pupil. It is ideal for recording where there are a large number of techniques and skills to master. Example 1 is limited in information, because it does not tell us how well the technique or skill is being done, and it does not distinguish between a pupil who has just managed to do it, perhaps in an 'easy-feed' non-competitive situation, and one who can produce it effectively under all conditions. Example 2 is still crude, there are no clear demarcation lines between categories in the sense of criteria, and no standardization

of pupils assessment (though teachers often do authenticate). Pupils often use a norm-reference system when terms like 'very good', 'good', 'poor' are used, instead of a criterion based on technique and skill. This is not helped sometimes by teachers who label the middle category as average. Example 3 which uses quality, quantity and context as criteria could be considered better. It means that pupils have to be made aware of the detail of the technique in order to complete it accurately and this will come from feedback from teachers or possibly other pupils. The method of ticking is mechanistic but easy to operate once the techniques and skills have been identified.

(b) Comment Banks

For the hard pressed PE teacher who has to write a lot of statements about hundreds of pupils, many of them similar because they use the same criteria, a way to cut down unnecessary duplication is essential. The use of comment banks has therefore been common. These are ready made statements which are selected as the most appropriate for each pupil. An example (table 24) is given from Skelthorne (1986), which was graded and computerized. The use of computers has made this system much more manageable and attractive to teachers because the range of comments can be widened. The difficulty in the past has been that the pupil has to fit in with the statements rather than the statements made to fit the pupil, and they often lacked the context which is against the DES 1989 statement of principles. They have often been developed on five-point scales like Skelthorne's, and contained negative comments which are not suitable for summative documents. Barden High School has tried to overcome some of these difficulties by devising a computer system which then summarizes the comment banks in a narrative form, putting in the context and personalizing the record. Figure 10 gives an actual example.

(c)   Bullseyes

This is where the record document uses a bullseye type target to show the level of achievement/skill. Munby (1989) gives examples from the University of Oxford in writing skills. Hatfield and Phillips (1989) at great Sankey Warrington used this system in some years to record personal qualities (figure 9). It serves the same purpose as ticking boxes as in figure 8, example 2, but may seem more interesting to the pupils in presentation. It is noted that at Great Sankey use is made of different forms of presentations for variety.

(d)   Open Boxes — Open Sentences

This is where open statements are made about targets but limited to space in a box. They are useful for asking the pupil to state targets or expectations such as, 'What can I do to improve?' (figure 9). Other boxes could have:

> I will be involved in . . .
> I will try to improve . . .
> I will work on . . .

They can also be useful to show achievements/qualities.

> The qualities I showed were . . .
> I made the most improvement at . . .
> My teacher and I feel I am good at . . .

Table 24: Selected comment banks from Skelthorne (1986)

Criteria	1	2	3	4*	5*
Equipped for lessons	Is always fully equipped	usually fully equipped	Occasionally is not fully equipped	often not fully equipped	Is rarely fully equipped
Interest and enthusiasm	Always works with interest, is a lively and eager participant	Normally shows interest and enthusiasm	Reasonably interested but without a great deal of enthusiasm	Does not show a great deal of enthusiasm	Shows no enthusiasm or interest in the subject
Ability to work with others	Can work extremely well with others, always makes a positive contribution	Usually works well in a group. Is able to share and contribute to the group	Can work well in a group but occasionally has difficulties	Tends to opt out when working with others	Does not contribute in any way in a group, is a nuisance and disrupts others
Games	Has a high level of skill, understands tactics and rules well	Has a good skill level and understands and applies rules	Is able to play a game with reasonable skill and applies the rules with guidance	Understands simple rules and has a limited skill level	Is unable to understand or apply rules and has difficulty with coordination
Fitness	Can keep up with physical exercise, takes regular exercise	Can keep up physical exercise but does not take regular exercise	Is not as fit as could be and sometimes has difficulty keeping going	Can not keep up with activity for long, tires easily	Is very unfit

* Not suitable for fifth year pupils as the nature of profiling should at this level be positive.

During this reporting session Philip has taken part in the following activities: football, basketball, rugby union, swimming, gymnastics and health and fitness. He has shown some interest but has not worked hard enough. Philip has maintained a reasonable level of participation but has only sometimes worn the correct kit. He has usually showered. His behaviour leaves something to be desired. We look for your support to improve this situation.

In games Philip has shown limited basic technique which he has used adequately in the game situation but he has understood most of the rules, tactics and procedures of play.

Philip can catch a ball. He can pass reasonably accurately. He has difficulty with basic control but can coordinate the basics of the set shot while shooting with some success. In rugby he can tackle in practice situations.

Philip has swum using front crawl. His technique is in need of improvement. He has entered the water by jumping feet first. He has understood the basics of water safety.

Philip can perform rotational movements, with support, both on the floor and apparatus and is able, with some assistance to work with a partner to produce a sequence of movements, balances. He has, to a greater extent, overcome his fear of heights.

Philip has shown some understanding of the 'S' factors and has demonstrated that he appreciates the relationship between diet, exercise and good health.

Figure 10: Specimen report on a year 7 pupil using comment banks but personalizing and contextualizing it (Barden High School)

(e) Grading

It has been very common to give a grading structure — usually a five point scale of A to E. Sometimes this has been given for an activity as a whole and includes one for performance and usually another grade for effort. More often though this grading system is used for PE as a whole, that is the grade represents a summary of the pupils' achievements and effort in all activities. As a criterion measure, like examinations, it suffers from aggregation problems and neglects individual contexts and is not very useful as a performance grade. It may be more useful as an effort grade if the pupil is consistent across contexts. The grading system is a 'relic' of the norm-referenced system, and the danger is that teacher and pupils are so used to norm-referencing that they continue to use it in this way. As we have seen a norm referenced system such as this means that some pupils will always be in lower categories and to progress it can only be at the expense of other pupils. To avoid this the criteria for each grade should be clearly stated on the document, such as in figure 11 and it could be related to activity contexts.

Whose Line Is It Anyway?

Pupil Recording

It is a principle of ROA that pupils should be involved in the assessing and recording of their own achievements and this is something which distinguishes it from the traditional school report (DES, 1984). However, it is possible for pupil

Attainment

A Very good techniques.
Maintains high level under competition

B Good technique.
Maintained most of the time under competition.

C Techniques adequate.
Breaks down some of the time under competition.

D Technique has limitations.

* Breaks down frequently under competition

E Basic technique deficient

* Not able to perform it under competition.

Effort

A Applied maximum effort always.

B Applies a lot of effort most times.

C Makes a good effort.

*D Inconsistent in amount of effort.

*E Little effort most of the time.

* Not suitable for summary document.

Figure 11: Suggestions for a criterion grading system

recording to take place with very little else changing. It would be easy enough to provide a tick list of skills in an activity for pupils to record without them really becoming involved in making judgments about themselves, making diagnostic assessments or realistic evaluations. Moreover, as we have noted the location and conditions in PE make recording difficult — playing fields, sports hall, gymnasium, weather, changing rooms. To get pupils really involved with their own assessments does involve a change in teaching style from traditional teaching. In PE the command type of teaching has been dominant (see Mosston, 1986) but the 'educational gymnastics' approach (see Smith, 1989) and games for understanding approach (Thorpe and Bunker, 1989) do involve a more pupil centred, reflective and decision-making approach. Apart from these areas, generally speaking pupils traditionally have not been asked to make assessments of themselves, and they have relied on those of the teachers. Consequently they can have difficulty in making accurate and useful assessments and recordings. My experience, and comments from other PE teachers, confirm the problems highlighted by the PRAISE report (DES, 1988), such as, superficiality, modesty, saying what their teacher seemed to want, and persistence of norm-referencing. The latter is particularly highlighted in PE because, unlike other lessons, in many of the activities the pupils are, in the context of the activity, in direct competition with other pupils, so other pupils' performances affects them directly. Furthermore, the pupils cannot see their own skills and techniques in action, except via video, nor, very often, the full game situation in team games. They need the feedback from an observer (teacher/coach). The problem is that the teacher cannot see all performances of all pupils or discuss them. It is both time consuming and impractical to have long discussions and reflections in the practical situation. There is a danger of destroying enthusiasm, flow and activity, and the teacher and pupil are in danger of being accused of an inactive lesson. Video recording can be useful in diagnostic assessment, but is impractical and costly to use all the time, and there is a need for technician or pupil operating the camera. However, it may be particularly helpful for GCSE and 'A' level PE.

There is no doubt that pupils will get better at self-assessment as they get used to being involved from a young age. However, one of the major difficulties is the power relationship between teacher and pupil, and this type of self-evaluation and recording does involve a change in the power structure, as Bernstein (1972) indicated some time ago. This change does pose difficulties for both teachers and pupils. It is expecting too much for pupils to make a complete change in their frame of reference overnight and it is the same for teachers.

There is usually a place for teachers to authenticate, sign, or make comments. If there is any serious discrepancy time must be found for discussion by the PE teacher. If time is limited for individual discussion and negotiation in PE (it is no different from other subjects), one answer to the problem is to deal with discussion and negotiation through the tutorial/pastoral system, where a teacher discusses all the areas on the record. This has advantages particularly where cross-curricular skills and personal qualities are involved which are not subject-specific.

PE teachers have found that continuous recording is not practical, and particularly as it takes time to master physical skills and to make progress in using them in more difficult or competitive situations. It is more usual and useful to record and target at the end of specific periods of time or modules, depending on the length, for example, half-termly. Sometimes specific tasks are set prior to recording, but, this must not prove too burdensome and time consuming. A balance must be struck between teaching time, assessment and recording time. PE teachers also have to contend with changing and showering which takes time at the beginning and end of lessons.

Confidentiality

One of the distinctive features of PE is its public face — what goes on, all pupils' performances, are open to view by other pupils and anyone else present. This is not the case with written work. Confidentiality is therefore a problem in PE. It is not easy for pupils to keep their shortcomings to themselves, and this can be acutely embarrassing to some children (low physical ability, uncoordinated, clumsy, those with particular fears of physical contact, heights, or going over apparatus, physical deformities, obesity, unfitness). In these cases diagnostic assessment and comments on performance, even if they are meant to be helpful, can exacerbate the situation. Recording can make things worse, because it might not be easy to record many 'ticks' in the achievement of skills. There can be little confidentiality where recording in changing rooms and PE locations, and discussion with teachers in PE context exists. Because PE teachers are used to this 'public face' of PE, they sometimes ignore the confidentiality issue. Problems of scrutiny are highlighted by PRAISE (DES, 1988) and Phillips (1989).

Equal Opportunities

Any document which recognizes the achievements of pupils inevitably differentiates pupils, and at the same time may possibly exacerbate any disadvantages. This can be the case with pupils of differing attitudes to ROA, those pupils of different abilities, gender, culture, social class, linguistic abilities, and it may also be reflected through the availability of activities outside school and the pupils' ability (economic and social) to avail themselves of them. The PRAISE document (DES, 1988) mentions some instances of this issue. Pupils in one school who lived in remote rural areas and less affluent homes had less opportunities available to them and so it showed on their ROA. Pupils from ethnic minority groups who had linguistic difficulties and were disadvantaged in teacher/pupil discussion and thereby on their ROA as a result. Differences between boys and girls approaches to ROA were also commented upon. Girls were generally more favourably disposed to ROA, were more diligent and less likely to record personal feelings, and seemed to value the intrinsic and formative record. The PRAISE report also raised the question of the sex of the teacher — whether it is preferable for pupils to be interviewed by teachers of the same sex. There was mixed evidence here, but the situation could be acute with Asian Muslim pupils. The sex roles of males and females in the Muslim community would suggest that it would be preferable if Asian children were interviewed by members of their own sex (see Carroll and Hollinshead, 1993a and 1993b).

So while PE teachers have, rightly in my opinion, welcomed the opportunity for pupils to record achievements in their subject, sporting participation outside school, and inter-school competition, it should be noted that whilst it enhances many pupils' records, it disadvantages others. The perceptive words of the PRAISE report should be heeded by all those enthusiastic PE teachers who commit themselves to extra-curricular activities.

> Although the rhetoric of ROAs emphasizes that positive recognition should be given to the way in which *all* pupils spend their time outside school, regardless of their social background, this ignores the powerful forces operating within schools which communicate to pupils the kinds of activities which are, and are not, acceptable. Notions of 'cultural deficit' are deeply ingrained, and teachers are quick to impose (unintentionally) those notions on pupils and to accept the reports by pupils from 'disadvantaged' or rural backgrounds that they do nothing out of school worthy of recording. On the other hand, teachers may be justifiably torn between their wish to draw out and give full recognition to their pupils' out of school achievements, and their concern that outside users of a ROA document may react negatively to description of activities which attract social disapproval. (p. 75)

It might be added that it also ignores the powerful forces which operate within communities which 'enable' and limit pupils' capacity to engage in the type of activity they do, for example, peer group interests and pressures to engage in activities such as pool and snooker, and types of music and dancing. Another example is parental and community influence on the status of leisure pursuits, which in the case of certain Asian Muslim groups devalue leisure pursuits for their children (Fleming, 1991). Carrington and Williams (1988) and Carroll and Hollinshead (1993a and 1993b) show the difficulty of Asian girls taking part in sporting and leisure pursuits after school, and boys' activities centering around the Mosque. Fleming (1991) and Carroll and Hollinshead (1993a) also comment on the effects of racism in pupils' attitudes to PE and leisure pursuits.

The PRAISE document does summarize by stating that as 'Evidence is slowly beginning to emerge of substantial differences between pupils of different sex, race and prior attainments in their approach and attitudes toward records of achievement' (p. 125). This needs to be looked at in relation to PE. Contrary to the PRAISE report, Jepson and Carroll (1991) found that girls did not report as favourably as boys on ROA and the effects on their learning and achievement. The authors report that this may be due to the subject, as generally girls are not as keen on PE and sport as boys, but this needs looking at further.

Accreditation and Validation

There has been some confusion and ambiguity in the use of these two terms, 'accreditation' and 'validation' as indicated by the PRAISE report (DES, 1988). The confusion is understandable in view of the close relationship between the two, and the need for the accrediting body to have validation procedures before they agree to certification. Thus it would be the purpose of validation to confirm that the correct principles and procedures are being carried out, such as whether the PE teacher carrying out the formative assessment procedures for each pupil has involved the pupil in the recording. The purpose of accreditation is to give it certification, authenticity and credibility outside the school. Accreditation by such bodies as the LEA and examination boards give that authenticity as in the Northern Partnership of Achievement (NPRA) and OCEA schemes.

The RANSC report (DES, 1989a) recommends that:

> the governing body of each school establish a records of achievement validation body which should consist of its own members, augmented from the local community and in particular from those representing and users of the record. The validation body will have to work within the national guidelines and accreditation principles which are set out below. (p. 19)

An example of validation showing aspects in PE is given in the PRAISE report (DES, 1988):

> For example, a PE department in one Dorset school set up a series of problem solving tasks to which pupils' leadership qualities were assessed and recorded in response to a validation board's view that the development of leadership qualities should be part of the curriculum. (p. 146)

This process of validation and accreditation is necessary for the summary document in order to give it credibility in the eyes of the public and the would-be users, employers and FE/HE institutes. The RANSC report goes on to recommend LEAs as the accreditation agency. Many of these have joined with examining boards as we have seen. In the NPRA scheme thirty-seven LEAs issued fifteen criteria which conform to the principles as laid down by the DES (1984 and 1989a). It gives more credence and motivation to the pupils. This is particularly valuable in PE where it was often thought that the achievements and personal qualities were not valued. The certification gives it that much more substance for both pupils, teachers and outside users. However, important as it is to get this credibility, and it will obviously have instrumental and motivational elements (after all, that was the purpose of ROA), the end product must not be given all the priority. It is the formative processes, the curriculum change potentiality of ROA which are equally as important. The internal validation bodies and procedures need to promote and sustain that change without being seen as 'external examiners'. Quality control needs to work in the same way as it should in staff appraisal, that is, leading to staff development. At the same time, for the pupil, ROA must not be seen as an additional surveillance or a social control mechanism as warned by Hargreaves (1989) and Broadfoot (DES, 1988). ROA in PE could be seen in these 'negative' ways because of PE teachers' interest in personal qualities and out of school activities. The development of assessment in the National Curriculum with its periodic assessment, which should be both diagnostic and feedback in purpose and formative in use should be part of the ROA and will strengthen the validation and formative phases.

Broadfoot (*ibid*) has commented on the conditions which are necessary for records of achievement to be successfully implemented. These include; the sense and ownership of the procedures, which sustains the belief in the value of ROA and commitment to them; the understanding of principles and commitment to them, practicability related to procedures, time and resources; credibility, which is more profound than the currency value and includes the acceptance of the principles and changes ROA should bring. The development of school and departmental policies which integrate assessment and recording into the curriculum as pivotal and central features rather than bolt-on procedures are essential. The reading of Broadfoot's synthesis and the PRAISE report (DES, 1988) is recommended.

Chapter 8

Assessment in the National Curriculum

Although this chapter will focus on assessment issues, these will be affected by basic curricular issues so some of these will be discussed. As the National Curriculum is in its early stages, it is necessary first of all to outline some of the basic requirements for the benefit of those in training and those coming new to the profession or returning to teaching.

The National Curriculum

The National Curriculum is established under the Education Reform Act of 1988. It comprises:

Three core subjects — English, mathematics and science.
Seven foundation subjects — technology (including design), history, geography, modern foreign languages, music, art and physical education.

Along with religious education and cross-curricular themes these provide a minimum curriculum.

In each core and foundation subject there are three components:

Attainment targets (AT) divided into ten levels of attainment (except for art, music and PE). These determine assessment objectives and state what pupils should know and understand, and what skills they should perform.
Programmes of study (POS) — define the teaching schemes syllabus.
Assessment arrangements — to determine what pupils have achieved.

PE, art and music have been treated differently from other foundation subjects and these differences will be discussed below. All the requirements will relate to *4 Key Stages (KS)* which relate to approximate ages of pupils and periods of schooling.

KS1	infant	5–7 years	years 1–2
KS2	junior	7–11 years	years 3–6
KS3	lower secondary	11–14 years	years 7–9
KS4	upper secondary	14–16 years	years 10–11

Assessment of pupils must take place before the end of each of the four key stages, and will require formal assessment, recording and reporting of the pupils' level of attainment. It is known that there will be a range of attainment at any given age or key stage so there will be an overlap of levels, for example, the range at 11 (KS2) might show levels 2–6. The GCSE will be the main form of assessment at key stage 4, but those pupils at key stage 4 not taking GCSE will be assessed. The National Curriculum POS and assessments are being phased in at different times by subject and key stages. PE entered the curriculum at KS1, 2, 3 in autumn 1992 and assessments will in autumn 1994. For the full timetable of implementation see DES (1989b) *From Policy to Practice.* For all subjects except art, music and PE, assessment will take the form of teachers' own assessments and standardised assessment tasks (SATs).

The Secretary of State for Education established working groups in each of the core and foundation subjects to recommend attainment targets and programmes of study. Interim and final reports were produced and sent for consultation within the teaching profession, and commented upon by the Secretary of State, the National Curriculum Council (NCC), and the Schools Examinations and Assessment Council (SEAC). The latter two bodies were required to engage in wide consultation. Both the NCC and SEAC have a wider remit and powers in relation to the National Curriculum and have produced a range of documents useful to teachers (see addresses in appendices). There is a different National Curriculum for Northern Ireland.

PE in the National Curriculum

The working party for PE is listed in appendix B of the interim report. (DES, 1991a). It consisted of thirteen members, including five who were not directly in education. The inclusion of non-PE members, and particularly famous sports people, does show PE's connection with sport, but this has been the subject of much criticism in the profession. However, it is noted in the final report (introductory letter) that some of these people were not able to attend all the meetings though they endorsed the report (DES, 1991b). It looks as if the structure of the content of the recommendations, for example, the three original attainment targets of planning, performing and evaluating which became components of the one attainment target and the breadth of the programme, are influenced more by the BCPE's working party (BCPE, 1989) and an educational approach than a competitive sportsman's approach.

The Secretary of State treated art, music and PE differently from other subjects. Instead of making *statutory* assessment of attainment targets into ten levels at the end of Key Stages, the working groups' remit for PE was to produce a 'single statutory statement of attainment expressed in broad terms for each key stage' (DES, 1991c, p. 3). The statutory statement of attainment at each Key Stage has become known as the End of Key Stage Statement (ES) whilst the statements of attainment into ten levels were to become *non-statutory*. The recommended programmes of study are *statutory*.

What this has done is to create three subjects of lower status in the foundation subject group. The Secretary of State has said that art and music will not be compulsory at Key Stage 4, but, fortunately, PE has avoided this. As the three subjects are 'practical' based subjects, doing and skill based, rather than 'academic', and already suffered from lower status in the traditional hierarchy, then this decision has reinforced the academic value in the National Curriculum. This was unfortunate as the introduction of the National Curriculum was an opportunity to attempt to put the practical subjects on an equal footing with other foundation subjects. The different treatment plus the fact that PE is in the last group of subjects to be phased in has meant that its timetable space in the curriculum has been squeezed and reduced in many schools. There is no stipulated amount of curriculum time for any subject, and there seems little doubt that those which place the greatest demands in terms of statutory assessment requirements, and which were in place first, will get priority. It seems certain that PE will suffer in this respect, because there is no minimum time requirement in the National Curriculum and nothing to say how long it will take to deliver the National Curriculum in statutory orders.

The good news about being treated differently from other subjects is that there is no requirement to carry out standard assessment tasks (SATs), which would have caused controversy. It is the SATs in the core subjects which have been most difficult to get right and caused the most problems so far in the primary school. More specific tasks at a given period would have been particularly burdensome to primary teachers. However the teacher still has to report at the end of key stages, and this has been made difficult by the presentation of the end of key stage statements in a single statement in broad terms as requested by the Secretary of State. The result is that there is only one part of one statement which is specific (swim at least twenty-five metres and demonstrate an understanding of water safety at KS2). Apart from this most of the statements are not very useful for assessment purposes. They do give a guide to the general objectives and dimensions on which to assess, but a statement such as, 'practise and improve performance', (KS1), is only useful as a *general* assessment objective, it lacks the more specific context and criteria which are required to make the assessment. Therefore, the teacher needs to turn to either the non-statutory levels suggested by the final report or the POS for more guidance. However, the Secretary of State did not make the ten levels statutory and therefore they have not been included in the final orders. Nor have they been included in the NCC non-statutory guidance (NCC, 1992). It is unfortunate that the Secretary of State took this line because then there would have been no need for general statements at the end of key stages, and the ten levels could have shown progression. This means the teachers must turn to the POS for the more specific context and criteria for assessment. However once again these provide a general context and criteria in the interests of flexibility of programmes. Specific contexts, criteria and tasks must be worked out by the teacher. Whilst teachers will welcome the NCC statement that 'assessment in physical education should not be unduly onerous' (NCC, 1992), the lack of guidelines at the present time is causing some anxiety amongst teachers and not just amongst primary non-specialists. It is these non-specialists who often need more detailed guidance in both POS and assessment as they lack the resources (human or other), experience, time and support which the secondary specialist can call upon. It is just as well that the NCC (1991) did not persist with the assessment of pupils on 'a three-point scale of below average, average and above average', as this would have been a return to norm referencing and confused teachers. Fortunately the NCC dropped this idea in their non-statutory guidance (NCC, 1992). The NCC, in its non-statutory guidance, did produce a useful diagram to show progression through the end of key stage statements, and highlighting planning, performing and evaluating as components of the attainment target (NCC, 1992, diagram 9). Figure 12 shows this diagram. Performing here applies to practical performance in the activity. As we have seen, this is a form of knowledge and understanding, and will also involve other forms of knowledge in different contexts such as laws in games, map and compass work in outdoor and adventure activities, basic physiology in health-related exercise, and community provision in developing programmes for active lifestyles. The presence of health-based programmes is welcome in view of its surprising absence in the rationale for PE in the final report (DES, 1991b, p. 5) (see Fox, 1992, for further criticism in this respect).

Although I suggested the ten levels would have been more useful for assessment purposes than the general End of Key Stage Statements, the ones proposed in the final report were not always adequate in wording, specific enough in context, or clear enough in its level appropriateness. To give some examples will show the difficulties of using general statements for assessment purposes:

show outstanding practical ability: (levels 9, 10)

Outstanding as a concept relating to other people is a norm-reference concept, whilst 'ability' is something which can only be judged from performance and would be risky to comment on in this context. It would have been better to have stated something like, 'show a high level of technical skill and application of skills, and tactics where appropriate, in practical performance' (types of activities). Like the general ES, this sort of statement still leaves the problem of the level of performance, and is repeated in a number of statements such as, 'show a depth of practical ability, knowledge and understanding in their chosen activities' (8), and 'improve performance through practice and rehearsal' (3), 'show that they are undertaking regular physical activity conducive to a healthy and enjoyable lifestyle' (8d). As it stands this latter statement can be met easily by any child taking part in regular physical activity outside the school, at a club or in class, so it would be met by a primary school child. Is regular participation really level 8? On the other hand, 'devise and carry out responses to tasks in changing a potentially hazardous environment taking account of their own and partner's skill' (5a), can be a very demanding task and reach higher levels than many of the statements, and makes high demands in terms of judgments, decision-making and evaluation skills.

What teachers have been left to do is to make assessments on the End of Key Stage statements. It has been left to the teachers to work out the level of pupils' performances and make comments on them. How this is actually done in the teaching context is dealt with in chapter 4 within setting the task and collecting the evidence. What it also entails in order for the assessment to be satisfactory is to develop good schemes of work, which incorporate the skills, knowledge and understanding and also show progression (see NCC, 1992). Examples of schemes showing progression are given in MacConachie-Smith (1991), health-related exercise in Harris and Elbourn (1992), games in Evans and Broll (1992), and in all areas in NCC (1992). If the appropriate schemes are introduced and appropriate tasks set to show different levels of performance, then the evidence

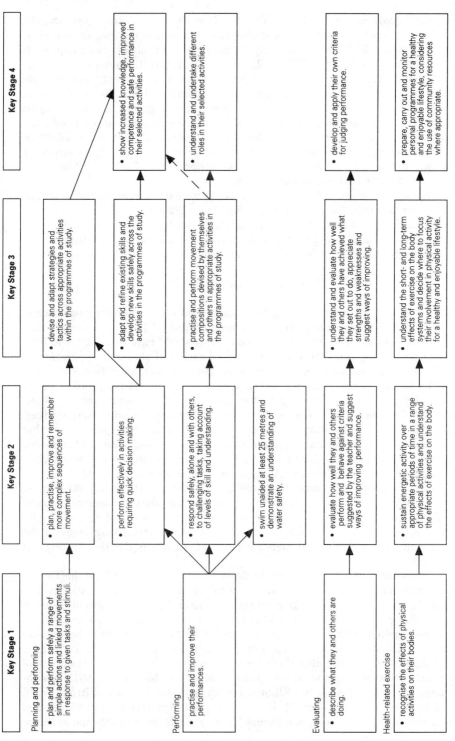

Figure 12:   Progression through the End of Key Stage Statements

will be there to make the judgments and the teacher will be able to report. What will *not* be there is standardization of teachers' assessments. There is a great deal of flexibility in the programmes of study for different contexts, introducing new activities as well as developing previously taught ones so there will also be flexibility in levels at each stage. The generality of the End of Key Stage Statements will lead to a great variety in the use of criteria and in the ways in which teachers assess, record and report. They may even lead to the job not being done precisely, or accurately enough, and perhaps glossed over quickly in the old school report syndrome manner by busy teachers, and those with less knowledge etc. The flexibility will be welcomed by many teachers and has its advantages. The variety of recording and reporting will not be a problem if it is well done, is based on a sound progressive programme and adequate criteria and if it is used formatively in teaching, and only summatively in respect of stating the level the child has reached. It will then only be a problem if a comparison is made between schools or LEAs as in league tables as recently happened in other subjects. Hence the need of SATs and teacher moderation in other subjects. Fortunately it does not appear that this will happen as PE does not have to report levels on the ten point scale. However, it would be useful if teachers in the same school standardized their criteria, assessments, recording and reporting so that it makes more sense to pupils and their parents.

The merging of the three ATs into one has made the End of Key Stage Statements more complex and multidimensional. Figure 12 shows that more than one component is included in many of the statements. Although progression is shown through the key stages there is no indication of level. Showing an increase of knowledge or performance is hardly a surprising or a useful statement. More detail would have been beneficial. Some of the statements will raise other issues too, for example, the monitoring of personal programmes and use of community resources, which are, on the surface, very commendable and indisputable objectives. However, they raise the question of equal opportunities and, perhaps, even personal liberties in the same way indicated in the discussion of ROA (see chapter 7). All pupils do not have equal access to community resources due to social circumstances and ethnic backgrounds. See, for example, the criticism of teachers by Sparkes (1991b) for ignoring social structure, and by Carroll and Hollinshead (1993a and 1993b) for ignoring ethnic cultural backgrounds in equal opportunities policies. Another issue is raised by the statement:

undertake a range of roles in the activities selected. (KS4)

Examples given are coach, umpire, player, choreographer, expedition planner and leader. Is to 'undertake' sufficient? Does standing in the field of play with a whistle on the odd occasion in a games lesson but not doing very much — is that sufficient to meet the requirements of an umpire or referee? How many roles should be undertaken? In fact, some of these roles can be very demanding for a child and present a serious challenge. This is particularly so when umpiring a competitive match, organizing and refereeing a complex tournament, choreographing a dance used in a show, planning and leading an expedition in hilly terrain. For too long in most schools the emphasis has been on performance/player role and these other roles have been neglected. Therefore this change is welcome, but more guidance would have been useful. The teacher will have to work out detailed criteria for these roles to give an adequate assessment. There are practical problems of time and equal opportunities. Will schools be able to cope with these adequately?

It is interesting to note that the Northern Ireland National Curriculum is different. Two Attainment Targets are included, Performance, and Appraising and Evaluating Performance, and ten levels on each AT have been included in the non-statutory orders. It will be interesting to see whether this works better than its English and Welsh counterpart.

The ten-level framework is required for the GCSE. Unfortunately in my view, the working group, in its wisdom, decided on a model that the National Curriculum requirements at KS4 and the GCSE would be different. The GCSE would be additional. So, it is not surprising that the original statements prepared in ten levels were not suitable for GCSE. The NCC also did not consider the 'level statements in their present form serve the purpose of defining an appropriate curriculum for KS4'. This means that either SEAC will have to produce a ten-level framework with statements of attainment incorporating the National Curriculum which the GCSE boards will have to work towards in revising their criteria, or they will have to produce their own.

GCSE and the National Curriculum

Carroll (1990a and 1991) has given a detailed analysis and discussion of the relationship and issues in the merging of the GCSE and the National Curriculum though they have been dated by the NCCs dropping of the 10 levels (NCC, 1991 and 1992). Substantially though the main issues pointed out remain the same. In the general requirements of *all* subjects:

(a) the equivalences between the GCSE scale and new ten levels as in table 19 will operate. It is proposed by the SEAC that descriptions of attainment at levels 4, 7 and 9 (at least) are included and these must meet the Attainment Targets. As mentioned above, the new ten levels in PE will probably be produced by the SEAC or the examining boards. In the GCSE at present it is the requirement to describe F and C only, though in PE some groups have described more than this, for example, SEG. These are attempts to replace the idea of grade-related criteria. (see chapter 6).

(b) Originally the SEAC criteria recommended that both coursework and examination work must contribute at least 20 per cent of the total marks, since then the Secretary of State has announced that there is a maximum amount of coursework, but this does vary according to the subject. There is no mention of PE, but all the syllabuses of the examining groups did comply with the original criteria. It would not appear to be appropriate for PE to be restricted in the amount of coursework. If this turns out to be the case, then it will also be a case of being glad PE is being treated differently (see chapter 6).

(c) GCSE syllabuses must match the relevant attainment targets, statements of attainment and programmes of study. So GCSE must incorporate the National Curriculum proposals. So now I will look at what GCSE has to do to do that.

The final report (DES, 1991b) and Statutory Orders (DES, 1992) recommended that the basic National Curriculum in PE consists of only two activities, which incidentally can be from the same group. Whatever happened to the concept of balance? It has clearly given way to the concept of specialism. Yet for GCSE, the final report recommended at least four activities from three areas, one of which must be gymnastics or dance. Why this should be is not stated. Although the NCC document (1991) makes the same statement regarding the basic curriculum, there is no mention of the GCSE, and there is no mention of the GCSE in statutory orders. I think it is necessary for the NCC and the SEAC to look at this carefully because there seems to be no justification for treating gymnastics/dance as compulsory. Only the WJEC syllabus meets this criteria. All the English and the NI syllabuses meet the concept of balance by grouping into different types of activities (see table 18) and gymnastics and dance is in an option block along with other activities such as athletics and swimming. Presumably the subject committees have grouped them like this according to their beliefs about balance, combined with practicality of carrying them out (facilities, staff expertise) and equal opportunities for the pupils to show what they can do. The new stipulation would upset that. At the present time, very few boys take dance (see table 16) and there are a limited number who take gymnastics so it might be thought that this recommendation favours girls. However, the National Curriculum for 5–14 gives a stronger basis in gymnastics or dance for both boys and girls and will give, in the future, a different foundation to the current situation for KS4. However Flintoff (1991) has shown that a lot of prejudices will have to be overcome for dance to become of more interest to males.

Another difference in the practical performance criteria in the National Curriculum is that the pupils must undertake different roles. The final report (DES, 1991c) made it clear that this included a wide range of roles such as umpire, coach, leader, but in the NCC (1991) report, only officiating is mentioned in the general examples, and in the more specific examples only 'different positions' are mentioned. The final orders (DES, 1992) state pupils must undertake different roles in their selected activities, and gives the example of:

> explain and demonstrate the role of choreographer in dance, a goalkeeper in hockey or a timekeeper in athletics.

However their place in the POS is not made clear. As mentioned above some of these roles are very demanding and they are also very time consuming. It does require a different approach to teaching and a broader view of PE than the traditional one. However, although many pupils do undertake officiating duties in GCSE courses as part of getting to know the rules, it has not been a demand in the criteria. Officiating is in fact not the same as 'Knowing the rules', although of course the latter is a prerequisite to effective officiating. Officiating demands in different activities are very variable, for example, contrast the demands of refereeing in basketball with umpiring in badminton. Because of the demands on time of pupils' officiating it may be necessary to start work on this aspect in the lower secondary school, and perhaps limit the number of activities it is required to officiate in at GCSE level, if it is to be done properly.

In the knowledge component comparison (see table 7), there is clearly a need for ULEAC and MEG to introduce knowledge and use of local community facilities into their syllabuses. This is worthwhile knowledge but difficult to assess in the examination situation. Coursework assignments seem the most appropriate method. However, it is in the component of evaluation which the GCSE has to make the most change. Although knowledge and understanding of techniques and skills and tactics are all part of the GCSE, there has been little attempt to examine evaluation. The pupils must now show that they can develop and apply criteria for judging performance and this has been discussed in chapter 4. The National Curriculum with its emphases on the processes of planning, performing and evaluating has placed much more emphasis on the evaluation aspect than the GCSE (see Carroll, 1991). The NEA's personal study does include the criteria of evaluation, but is not related to practical performance, only to the research and the study itself.

In my view it would have been better if the working party had seen GCSE and the KS4 level as the culmination of secondary schooling in PE as it has been in other subjects. This would have meant that KS4 would have been more substantial and provided a wider basis of knowledge and performance than the current restricted KS4. This now appears to be half a course. It also means that the GCSE, and therefore the full programme, is optional. If the GCSE and KS4 had been seen as the same all pupils would have done the wider programme, but not all would necessarily have had to be entered for the examination. Now there has to be two programmes.

Can the National Curriculum in PE be Delivered?

This is really asking can the National Curriculum be delivered effectively, satisfactorily and in the very spirit of the working groups' intentions? It is one thing to effect a law, it is quite another to make it effective in practice. But why should there be any difficulty in delivering the National Curriculum programme and assessments? There are grounds for believing there will be difficulties.

Primary Level

I think the most concern lies in the primary school, where there are few resources and facilities and little staff expertise. The lack of specialist PE teachers in the primary sector has often led to fragmented programmes, lack of continuity and progression in the children's work, not being up to date with new developments in the subject, and low priority for resources. Trainee teachers, including those with limited background and little personal interest in the subject, could spend as little as twenty hours in a PGCE course, and have a limited number of lessons teaching the subject on teaching practice. In the past the primary class teacher always 'burdened' by the wide range of subjects he/she has had to cope with has found little time for INSET. Now 'overburdened' by the National Curriculum, the amount of new material in many of the subjects such as in science, and assessment arrangements, the teacher is going to find it even more difficult to find time for INSET in PE. There appears to be little doubt that the National Curriculum is making new demands on primary school teachers.

In view of what I have just said about the primary sector, it is perhaps not surprising that in both the reports of PE inspections in the 1980s (DES, 1991c) and the joint survey of primary schools by the Central Council for Physical

Recreation (CCPR) and National Association of Head Teachers (NAHT) (CCPR, 1992), there are grounds for serious concern over whether the National Curriculum can be delivered adequately. The Inspection Review (DES, 1991c) findings show that:

> In one quarter of the schools, PE did not receive sufficient emphasis.
> One third of the lessons seen were not satisfactory.
> Work generally was most suitable to average ability only.
> In junior schools, playing major team games took a disproportionate amount of time and emphasis at the expense of the development of skills, small sided games, dance and gymnastics. In the infants' sector, limited attention was paid to games skills and pupils were set unsuitable tasks. Opportunities for creative dance and movement as an art form were rare and movement lessons using radio broadcasts were unrelated to other lessons.
> Inappropriate use of award schemes in some schools.
> A failure to share professional ideas.
> Most schools had a deficiency in facilities in at least one area, for example, one third in shortcomings of indoor space, one third in hard surface areas. This deficiency is supported to some extent by the CCPR/NAHT survey (CCPR, 1992).

It is quite clear though that many teachers did not help the situation and needed basic help in planning programmes when the following is read in the report,

> Records of progress in physical education were kept in about one quarter of the schools. In the majority of the schools the important links between planning, schemes of work, assessment and record keeping were not developed in ways which would help the teachers plan progression'. (DES 1991c, p. 13)

However, it is also clear that it is very difficult for curriculum leaders to do their job properly when conditions do not allow them time to do the job properly, for example,

> Teachers with curricular responsibility for the subject often found it difficult to influence the overall quality of the work because there was no time to observe other classes being taught or to work alongside their colleagues. Similarly, time could not be found for other teachers to observe the 'work of those responsible for the subject'. (p. 13)

Swimming was reported on favourably in the inspection review though it was pointed out that very few primary teachers had swimming qualifications and that teaching was carried out by specialist instructors employed at the public baths by the local authority (DES, 1991a). However, this has to be paid for out of the education budget, and the costs, including travelling, are increasingly being thrown on to individual schools. The Sports Council (1991) has thrown doubt on the adequacy of provision of swimming pools for schools to deliver the National Curriculum in swimming and highlighted the need and cost of maintaining and updating existing facilities, and the desirability of local authorities continuing to pay for the cost of swimming instruction to spread the cost. The CCPR/NAHT survey shows that 25 per cent of schools which replied did not have access to a swimming pool (CCPR, 1992). Meeting the swimming requirements could be a problem for some schools.

The CCPR/NAHT survey was a national survey of all primary schools. Although only 15 per cent replied, this was a total of 3,236 and still represents a significant number of schools, teachers (30,078) and pupils (717,496). Of all the teachers in these schools, only 8 per cent had formal PE qualifications, and 86 per cent of the headteachers commented on the need for in-service training. The survey supported the Inspection Review findings on the inadequacy of facilities in some schools, for example, 7 per cent had no indoor space available and in 27 per cent the indoor space was too small to carry out the activities adequately, only 2 per cent had access to sports halls or gymnasia and 16 per cent had no access to a sports field. The survey also revealed other concerns, which throws doubt on the adequacy of National Curriculum provision, such as a reduction of time available for many of the activities in the order of 12 per cent, and 40 per cent of schools had no PE budget, and where one was available the majority had set a 'per capita allowance of £1 per year'. It is not surprising then that 51 per cent of Parent/Teachers Associations gave money to supplement the PE budget.

If the Inspection Review and CCPR survey give a representative picture, and I suspect they do, there is cause for concern. The National Curriculum has not come too soon and should be welcomed. Now, according to the law, there will be a National Curriculum for ages 5 to 16 with balance, continuity and progression. However the drawing up of National Curriculum programme and assessment arrangements are clearly not sufficient to overcome the shortcomings shown above, and there is doubt as to whether it can be delivered. It is the teachers who have to carry out the programme, and need the resources and facilities to do so. Changes of this proportion do not happen overnight. In fact, recent events have exacerbated the situation and made it more difficult for primary teachers to deliver the National Curriculum, such as:

(a)   the demands made on teachers by the National Curriculum in other subjects — new material for the teachers to teach, for example, science, and the assessment arrangements which have been controversial and demanding;

(b)   funding arrangements to LEAs and schools have limited funding for resources and INSET. Money for travelling to recreational facilities such as fields and swimming baths has been cut, or prices of travelling and facilities gone up. Many LEAs have put the onus on schools to pay for these things themselves. Many LEAs have cut their specialist advisory support services. This is a pity because the Inspection Review (DES, 1991c) quoted above pointed out that much of the best work and INSET was prompted or promoted by advice and support from LEAs.

The National Curriculum in PE is going to make extra demands on the teacher and the school in terms of balance and breadth of knowledge and curriculum and in terms of expertise and greater in-depth knowledge required. Teachers may make an attempt to meet the National Curriculum and the letter of the law, but what will be the result? Many teachers felt uncertain in their knowledge and expertise (*ibid*) in the limited main areas already existing, particularly gymnastics and dance, so to broaden the range to include outdoor activities might result in another area where the teacher is uncertain, resulting in poor quality teaching.

Generally the teaching quality will not suddenly change because of the National Curriculum and if there is a fundamental change to be made, for example, in teaching style, in organization, in planning, and in assessment, then there will be considerable difficulties (see Sparkes, 1991a).

In order for the National Curriculum to be delivered effectively in the primary sector, a number of things will have to be done. Some of these can be identified through the examples of good practice in the Inspection Review (DES, 1991c).

(i) Whilst the primary class teacher who teaches most of the subjects to the class exists, it is necessary to appoint a teacher who acts also as curriculum leader for PE in each school. These teachers should be specialists or have some degree of training and expertise in the subject, with a job description to include this aspect. The leader must be given time to advise and work with other teachers and the children to enable teachers to see good practice in action, and to share professional ideas.

(ii) The appointment of specialist advisers in PE to support the curriculum leaders and all teachers. The decline in the numbers of advisory teachers needs to be halted now at the introduction of the National Curriculum where there is most work to be done. There are some outstanding examples of exemplary work done through LEA advisory service.

(iii) The curricular leaders and advisory service must improve the teachers' knowledge and understanding of requirements of the National Curriculum, activity-specific knowledge, and also planning schemes with progression in assessment and recording of performance.

(iv) Adequate resources and facilities are necessary for the effective carrying out of the curriculum. It is clear that an effort must be made to give the resources and facilities to where they are needed. Perhaps the National Curriculum can make a case for extra funding, but with the present government this seems unlikely. Mr. Clarke (the then Secretary of State) seemed particularly concerned about demands for extra resources in his communication to the working group (DES, 1991b).

One of the effects of the National Curriculum may be the introduction of more specialist subject teachers in the primary school. If this is extended to PE then it would be in the best interests of the children and high quality standard of work throughout the school. If primary PE is not put on a sound footing then the whole concept of the 5–16 curriculum based on balance, continuity and progression is in danger. The secondary schools will have to pick up the pieces as they often do now.

Secondary Level

There should be fewer problems for the secondary schools, as they have the PE specialists and superior facilities. The NCC (1991) and the final orders (DES,

1992) made it easier for schools to deliver the balance in KS3 than the final report (DES, 1991b) by recommending that pupils have to cover four out of the five activities and not the full five activities (athletics, dance, games, gymnastics and outdoor adventure activities, whilst swimming was merged into other categories). It will be a relief to many boys and male staff that dance does not have to be covered, but, of course, this will do nothing to attack its feminine image (see Flintoff, 1991). However, outdoor pursuits could well be a problem for some schools as they requires specialist staff. Many PE teachers do not have the expertise or the qualifications to teach these activities, and they are also time consuming and difficult to fit into the curriculum timetable for most schools. Many local authorities demand specialist qualifications to take children on adventure activities into mountainous areas or on water for safety and insurance reasons. A number of notable accidents prompted this move in LEAs. Therefore outdoor activities are often carried out at a specialist outdoor centre run by the LEA and are usually residential. There are two problems in carrying out the National Curriculum in this way. First, the cost — who will pay? Secondly — the centre will not be able to cope with all pupils in a local authority. It can only be on an optional basis as at present. This means that a favoured few, as at present, can take advantage of the LA provision and at the same time cover an area in the National Curriculum. But for most pupils, the school will have to do it locally. This will still present problems of time, staff expertise and availability, staff student ratios, travel and cost. For some very favourably located schools with suitably qualified staff this may be possible. This will only leave the problem of cost, though the equal opportunities issue is bound to crop up again for the socio-economically disadvantaged. If outdoor activities are not covered then clearly all the other areas will have to be over the two years, which means dance for boys. Facilities may be a problem in some poorly endowed schools, particularly inner city schools and time and money must be spent on travelling.

Swimming is only included in the National Curriculum as a separate activity up to KS2, but it can be continued after that stage. The effect of this could be to reduce the amount of swimming in the KS3 and 4 particularly where cost and travelling are involved. The Secondary Heads Association (SHA) survey with a sample of 1582 schools showed that swimming in the state sector had decreased in 23 per cent of the schools over the last ten years and increased in only 6.5 per cent of the schools (SHA, 1990). The same survey revealed that only 35 per cent of the state schools had sole or dual use of a swimming pool. The Sports Council survey (1991) on swimming pool provisions lends support to the belief that swimming may decrease further in state schools.

One of the things the National Curriculum will do is to achieve balance. As the SHA survey (1988) shows that athletics and games are included in the curriculum at all ages in the majority of schools and some form of gymnastics in a high percentage of schools, then it will come down to a choice between dance and outdoor pursuits as the fourth compulsory activity. However if the choice is between outdoor pursuits and dance at KS3, they do cover very different aspects of the child's education and curriculum objectives. They are not true alternatives. They do have gender biases too (see Flintoff, 1991; Humberstone, 1992). These gender biases are reflected in the entry figures for GCSE (see table 6) and in the SHA survey (1990). Although in the latter report it is not clear from the tables of mixed secondary schools whether activities are taught to both girls and boys, the statistics of single sex schools are revealing and shows clear gender biases. Table 25 shows figures of dance and outdoor pursuits extracted from the SHA survey (1988) of single sex state schools. It is not clear what outdoor pursuits includes as skiing, orienteering, canoeing and rock climbing are also listed separately and these have been averaged in table 25. It is suggested that, although in mixed schools there is more likelihood of a higher percentage of boys taking part in dance and girls in outdoor pursuits, nevertheless the trend suggested by the SHA survey is most likely to be repeated and particularly at KS3.

At the present time the secondary school curriculum is often accused of imbalance. In boys' PE and in male departments there is a preponderance towards games, whilst gymnastics has declined, and dance is almost non-existent. Girls' PE tends to be better balanced. Many PE teachers will obviously have to examine their own practices and overcome their own biases and prejudices to achieve the balance. Many teachers, even though they are specialists, would feel uneasy about teaching and assessing in some of the areas, for example, males in dance and gymnastics, but if there is not sufficient expertise in the department, and in a small school this is a distinct possibility, then some professional development will be required.

Clearly what is required is for the teacher to plan schemes of work in the light of National Curriculum arrangements and build in appropriate assessment tasks and recording mechanisms (see chapters 4, 5 and 7).

The purely recreational type programme in the upper secondary school, which in effect meant just playing a game with no emphasis on teaching or progression, is no longer good enough for the era of National Curriculum and accountability. In fact, it never was good enough, but some PE teachers 'got away with this' curriculum, which may be a relic from the era of when extra-curricular tended to receive the most attention in PE.

Will the National Curriculum Raise Standards?

The National Curriculum as a whole was brought in on the ubiquitous concern about falling standards and accountability. So will it raise standards in PE? It depends upon what one means by standards. Does it mean the standards of the very best performers (elitist view), or the overall standards of pupils? The 'elitist' view which concentrated teaching/coaching and resources on the best performers, very often in extra curricular activities, did in fact, in many schools, provide very high standards for a few pupils. But it was very often at the expense of the majority. The specialist tradition and competitive attitude and programme outside of the school curriculum, and sometimes within it, plus perhaps additional play at clubs, gave the best pupils many opportunities to reach high standards. This tradition was attacked by the school teachers' 'industrial' action in the mid-1980s, and further eroded by changes in philosophy, that is towards egalitarianism and anti-competition (see Pollard, 1988). This 'new' philosophy and 'new' programmes were regarded as an attack on elitist attitudes and traditional standards, and in fact, many people regarded standards as having fallen during the 1980s (BBC *Panorama*, 1987). At the same time there was a concern over the fitness standards of pupils (*ibid*; Armstrong, 1990). What the introduction of CSE, GCSE and Health Related Fitness programmes did was to renew the focus on the

Table 25: Number and percentage of single sex schools in the SHA Survey (1988) participating in dance and outdoor pursuits

	11+ Boys		11+ Girls		12+ Boys		12+ Girls		13+ Boys		13+ Girls		14+ Boys		14+ Girls		15+ Boys		15+ Girls		Total Average Boys		Total Average Girls	
	No	%	No	%	No	%	No	%	No	%	No	%	No	%	No	%	No	%	No	%	No	%	No	%
Dance (Med Ed)	4	6	63	75	3	4	70	74	1	1	62	61	0	0	42	41	0	0	36	35	1.5	2	51	57
Dance (Folk, Other)	0	0	17	20	0	0	15	16	0	0	13	13	0	0	16	16	0	0	15	15	0	0	15	16
Outdoor Pursuits	11	15	5	6	12	16	7	7	25	30	14	14	29	34	21	21	30	35	18	15	21	25	13	12
Outdoor Pursuits (four specific activities averaged)	10	14	3.5	3.5	14	18.5	5	5.5	18	22	9	9	20	26	11.5	11.5	21	26	11	11.5	14.5	24	8	10

curriculum, and in the examination courses the pupils worked to higher standards and increased their knowledge, understanding and performance in a way that was never attempted in non-examination courses. What was happening was, that whilst the quantity and possibly the quality of extra-curricular activities were in decline, the curriculum was being broadened and the quality within the curriculum was being raised, particularly in examination courses. This may of course be regarded as replacing one elitist group with another as far as raising of standards is concerned. However, the National Curriculum is attempting to raise the standards for all pupils throughout all the stages of their school life. If the basis can be effected in the primary sector there should be a better balance, continuity and progression than there is now. However, the problems for the primary schools have been noted, and these must be tackled if a satisfactory basis is to be achieved. Eventually, this will mean a better foundation to start the secondary programme than there is at present. What we should see is overall higher standards by many more pupils in a wider range of activities by the end of KS3, and then in the basic National Curriculum KS4 (non-GCSE) an opportunity for them to take some activities to a higher standard, try different roles, and make links within the community. This will not come automatically. It will only come about if teachers are willing to make it happen, and for those who need to change to effect that change and not to carry on in the same way. Many PE teachers will find the National Curriculum no problem as they are already working at the quality encouraged in the National Curriculum.

The National Curriculum is an assessment-driven curriculum, and the Government appears to believe that this type of curriculum and assessment does raise standards (for example, DES, 1989a). As Gipps (1990) has stated there is no real evidence to show that an assessment-driven curriculum actually raises standards. It does usually result in teaching to the assessment narrowing of the curriculum and an improvement in test results to a given limit. However, the Government has also introduced 'high stakes' assessment through the publication of results (*ibid*). What we have now is an aim for above minimal level competency, an attempt for maximum competency (*ibid*). This will tend to raise standards. Physical education is not quite in the same position as other subjects as AT levels cannot be published and therefore cannot be included in league tables. The assessment arrangements for PE will not automatically raise standards. The general ES are such that they will not push up standards as the GCSE might well do with its grades of competency and marking systems. However, the National Curriculum could be used to raise standards if formative assessment takes priority over the summative, and by making pupils aware of criteria and competency, by targeting, by good curriculum design and arrangement of tasks to appropriate levels of difficulty (see chapter 4). If the summative-formative conflict which might well occur in the 'high standards–high stakes' philosophy in other subjects is not prominent, then the assessment can be both usefully used by both teacher and pupil in diagnosis of strengths and weaknesses and used to direct teaching. This is what has always been at the heart of good teaching and learning. What should result is a raising of standards for all pupils, not just the elite, or one particular group. Neither should the best performers be neglected. Very often teaching in curricular time is aimed at the average performers, the best are not always challenged, the weakest are sometimes left to 'flounder'. The National Curriculum hopefully will change that, but it will require a determined attempt by teachers to do so, to increase their own knowledge, and to look at their teaching methods and assessment practices. Effective assessment of pupils will give the evidence to show standards of pupils' performance and whether standards are being raised.

Chapter 9

Consequences and Effects of Assessment

Educational Identity

Throughout the chapters of this book I have been concerned with the purposes and uses of assessment. The importance of the purpose has been highlighted as basic to the what, how and when assessment takes place within the broad formative-summative dichotomy. The relationship of assessment to teacher and school accountability, to pupil motivation, and to elements of social and quality control, are stressed as fundamental features of assessment arrangements and particularly in the new initiatives such as the National Curriculum and ROA. However, in attempting to achieve the purposes and in utilizing assessment practices and results, there are often latent and unintended consequences of assessment. Some unintended consequences are readily seen and experienced, such as the examination 'industry' and the bureaucratic procedures needed to sustain it. These are deemed necessary and unquestioned in the search for fairness, justice, standardization and comparability. However, there are other not so obvious consequences of assessment such as expectations and labelling, and the pervasive nature of assessment and evaluation in teachers' and pupils' lives (Carroll, 1976a). Much of the work looking at expectations and labelling has not been done directly in relation to assessment, although it is, in effect an assessment of the child and consequences of it. It has tended to be divorced from assessment, for example, Hargreaves work on labelling with its roots in deviance theory (Hargreaves, Hester and Mellor, 1975), and Nash's work on expectations (Nash, 1973).

Carroll (1986b) makes the link more directly than most between labelling and assessment:

> Labelling is a complex process, and at its heart is an assessment of pupils in the teachers' care. Assessment is an in vogue concept at the moment and is acceptable. An analysis of the labelling process does give us clues as to how the teacher assesses pupils, and this study has shown some of the cues, criteria and consequences of the teachers' assessment and identification. So 'what's in a name?' It means clear identification and status with its resulting consequences, either negatively or positively. It is both a resource and a framework for pupil action. It is more than a mere label. (p. 27)

Carroll portrays labelling as an educational identity making process, firmly based in a socially constructed world (see Blumer, 1971) of the classroom, gymnasium and playing fields. The public nature of the situation, such as the open display of pupil-teacher interaction in the teaching context or the publication of examination results enhances the identity creating properties. But, the real significance of the social process of identification lies in how the identity or label is used by both teachers and pupils as a basis for inferences about pupils. This is how teachers explain pupils' actions, legitimate accounts and hold expectations of behaviour and performance. What it means, in effect, as Carroll (1986b and 1986c) shows is that an identity is created for the pupils such as, the 'Troublemaker', 'Skiver', 'Athlete', 'Sportsman', 'Enthusiast', 'Star', 'Bright', 'Thickie', on the criteria of ability, attitude and behaviour. What can happen is that pupils are always seen within the framework of their 'identity', and the pupil becomes a particular type in the eyes of the teacher and other pupils. Behaviour and ability are seen in the light of that 'identity'. First impressions and early evidence are important in the formation of identities in the 'speculative' and 'elaborative' phases (Hargreaves *et al*, 1975). Later evidence in the 'confirmation' phase does just that, it confirms that identity. Expectations can become very strong and prove a limiting framework within which pupils are seen and within which they can work. Reputations are formed and can lead to living up to the reputation. This can be both positive and negative, but be most destructive to the pupil in the case of the 'Troublemaker' (Carroll, 1986c). Reputations can even precede pupils on transfer from junior to secondary schools, and this may be exacerbated when a full ROA and National Curriculum are in place. Reputation can even affect brothers and sisters, and is known as the 'sibling phenomena' (Hargreaves *et al*, 1975). This can have negative consequences for pupils if older siblings have a bad reputation, or if they have to try to live up to very high standards of their elder siblings.

Teacher expectations can cause self-fulfilling prophecies, in which original false perceptions become true. The self-fulfilling prophecy is based on Thomas' dictum, 'If men define situations as real, they are real in their consequences' (Thomas, 1928). The research work of Rosenthal and Jacobson (1968) using IQ scores and Douglas (1964) reporting on streaming by ability does indicate that teacher expectations can effect pupils' performances. Although Rosenthal and Jacobson have been criticized, and there are alternative explanations of Douglas' work, enough work has been done to accept the general principle (Rowntree, 1977). However, some of researchers are like magicians — they do not explain how it is done. However, it is clear that it does not work in mysterious ways, it can only be through the interaction processes, either through ephemeral clues in the teaching-learning situation where the teacher conveys his/her impressions of the pupil, expectations and judgments, or, through unconscious or conscious differential treatment, such as the amount of contact time, groupings etc. This is how gender, class and ethnic group differentiation, expectations and stereotyping work, as well as those based on ability and behaviour.

Some studies have shown that teachers' frameworks are important in providing the framework in which pupils have to show their ability and do provide a limitation on what counts as ability (Barnes *et al,* 1971; Keddie, 1971; Hammersley, 1974). Although there are no specific studies directly related to ability in PE, it can be applied to teachers' views as to what is regarded as technical competence and tactical awareness in physical activities and teachers' perceptions of positional play and types of players in games, and what counts as legitimate knowledge in theoretical and practical work. Examples in PE might be:

(a) In an activity like tennis where the teacher's perceptions of what counts as good technique when clearly professional players exhibit different techniques and styles of play, not all of which have been accepted as 'good' in the past.

(b) The acceptance of rugby union, rugby league or soccer as the appropriate game to play (see Jackson and Marsden, 1962), or perhaps snooker or darts as illlegitimate activities and physical abilities. This does have a bearing on assessment within the National Curriculum, the GCSE and for ROA.

(c) 'Who fits into the team' in extra-curricular activities, the 'halo' affect of smart appearance and middle-class backgrounds, the stereotyping of male and female behaviour (see Evans, 1989; Scraton (in relation to PE), 1986) and ethnic minorities (see Bayliss, 1989; Carrington and Wood 1983 in relation to PE).

The research work of Ball (1981), Hargreaves (1967), Keddie (1971) and Lacey (1970) amongst others show the significance of organizational structures such as ability groupings of pupils on their educational identity resulting in differentiated knowledge and teaching. These studies have shown the polarization of culture resulting from organizational structures and the possible polarized careers. Quite clearly organizational structures and cultures have a profound effect on pupils, their identity and their assessments. The contrasting cultures produce pupils who identify with the school and their aims, and those who would like to disassociate themselves entirely. As one pupil said, 'it may be all marble, but I won't swim for the bloody school' (Hargreaves, 1967). Although these researches were carried out some time ago and schools have learned some of the lessons in terms of pupil groupings and organization, the assessment and examination system produces structures which do alienate many pupils from school, and there are many pupils disaffected by the system, particularly in the inner city areas. The National Curriculum may, in fact, influence and produce different organizational structures, such as setting according to levels rather than age with ability, and specialist subject teaching in junior schools, the effect of which we are not yet sure about. The National Curriculum with its emphasis on testing at key stages and a broad range of academic subjects, even after Key Stage 3 may do nothing to further the integration of disaffected children into the school and may well alienate them further. A combined route with vocational training was clearly rejected by the government, which may have done something to alleviate the problem.

The work of Hargreaves *et al* (1975), Bird (1980) and Wood (1981) suggests that pupils do give legitimacy to teachers' identification of pupils and labels, particularly on the academic side, but the context is important. The consequences of being identified as a given type have been shown by Carroll (1986b and 1986c). For example, the consequences of being labelled as an 'athlete', (high physical ability in a wide sense) have meant in many cases, extra encouragement, attention, and recognition given to the pupil and more time being spent on the activity, and possibly, receiving more high level coaching. Thus the pupil receives differential treatment, and is more likely to use and realize his/her ability and to progress at a faster rate. Giving pupils equal opportunity if they show their ability does not mean equal treatment. However, this has often meant that it only applies to a narrow range of activities, that is, the ones in which the school has sporting fixtures, inevitably this means the major games. Many 'athletes' therefore remain 'undiscovered'. The National Curriculum could help to change this by the broader range of activities now offered below stage KS3, and its encouragement of sporting links with the community (see DES, 1991b, appendix C, pp. 67–74).

The main consequence of being labelled a 'troublemaker' has been that the pupils were constantly being watched, and at the first sign of being out of line they were 'jumped upon' (Carroll, 1986a). Their behaviour was likely to be treated as deviant on the basis of past identification of behaviour and the pupils' motives and intentions inferred from it. Often it was difficult to change type because the teacher inferred particular motives and intentions and also because the causes were seen to lie in the home, upbringing or social conditions.

Competition and Control

Giving pupils an 'identity' in PE is necessary and functional. The teacher cannot avoid the assessments or the categorizations. It appears to serve a very important function of differentiating between pupils on different criteria and giving the teachers a framework for expectations and action. It does, however, have consequences for the pupils, some negatively unfortunately, but many positively. However teachers can avoid stereotyping pupils along ability and behavioural dimensions as well as class, ethnicity and gender dimensions. They can avoid neglecting individuality too, but this can be difficult when dealing with whole classes and larger groupings where individual needs have to give way, in many instances, to the larger group needs. A well run programme with a good system of ROA should help the teachers to avoid the difficulties to some extent, by getting to know the individual pupils better, what they are capable of, and how they are progressing. By emphasizing the individual nature of assessment, self-referencing, and progress against own previous performances, the intense competition that is prevalent in PE and the assessment system can be modified. The activities themselves are intensely competitive and this is an essential ingredient of PE, so pupils inevitably measure their performance against others. However, the assessment itself should not be competitive, it should be seen as part of a learning environment. Further competition has been introduced into the system at the school and LEA level by the Government's publication of National Curriculum results and GCSE results. Thus we find that school is pitted against other schools in the area (regardless of neglecting all the contributory factors to such results), and Richmond LEA is held up as an example to Bradford LEA in a public accountability exercise. The LEA results, we are told by the Government, had nothing to do with socioeconomic background, or, with members of ethnic minority children from homes where English is a second language, or, with the amount of money spent by an LEA. The comparability exercises conveniently neglected to look closer at the standardization of teachers' marking and socio-economic factors, and that these results were supposed to be 'unreported SATs' at that stage. The Government has introduced the 'high standards-high stakes' philosophy mentioned in the previous chapter. What this type of exercise is going to do is to intensify pressure at the classroom level to get better results. Schools are going to show that they have better results than before, and than their neighbouring schools in marketing exercises. 'Creative statistics' will become fashionable. PE will not avoid this, because the philosophy will pervade the whole school. The PE teachers will not have to report levels of the National Curriculum results for publication, but GCSE results will be included in the league tables. Moreover the 'market forces' philosophy which has been applied to the education service will exacerbate the situation and influence schools and PE in other ways, such as the use of the rates of attendances, participation rates in school sports, sports results, provision of sports facilities etc. The presentation and marketing of all aspects may become more important than what is actually going on. The danger is that the reputation and label may serve the school better than the content and process (educational) as very often happens with many wines in the wine trade. Attention may well be drawn to facts and figures, and in assessment the emphasis may well drift away from the formative processes to the summative product. The gains that could be made through the National Curriculum and ROA to the pupils, to the teaching-learning situation could be lost in the emphasis of the summative product. That would be an unfortunate consequence of the government's actions in the search for accountability. This is not to deny the value of the summative product or assessment but to emphasize the dangers of particular consequences of uses.

The Place of Assessment in Schools in Society

Most of what I have been writing about has been about the educational and technical aspects of assessment, and it is perfectly possible to operate in the classroom at that level without further understanding of its place and function in schools or society. But operating at this level does not prevent the teacher being 'used' by the system or a 'pawn' in political and ideological functions. To really have a fuller understanding and to get to know what this thing called assessment is all about, one needs to understand these political aspects and how assessment fits into the ideologies of society. This is a complex issue but one I must draw attention to, although I cannot fully do justice to it here. It is something which is usually neglected in books on assessment, the notable exception being Broadfoot (1979). One might suggest that the assessment reforms of the 1980s have brought home the political nature of educational initiatives in a way they have not done so since the abolition of the 11+ examination and the introduction of the comprehensive school. But this is the 'open' and obvious political face of the relationship, and there are deeper, 'hidden' explanations of the relationship and functions in society.

Teachers are familiar with the differentiation-selection functions of education and examinations, in particular, how they serve both education and employment, and the overpowering nature of the resulting system upon the curriculum and the way pupils are perceived and assessed. It is a competitive system that values academic attainment above all else. It is a system which has remained impervious to change in spite of reform. In fact most educational reforms in the recent past, the 1944 Education Act, the abolition of the 11+ and the advent of comprehensive schools, the introduction of the CSE. and later the GCSE, strengthened the system. The latest, the National Curriculum with its concern for standards, will do the same. This is because the reforms are based on a philosophy and ideal of equal opportunity for 'merit'. Ability is the 'new privilege' and replaces the old privilege of birth. However, it is a particular and limited scale of ability, one where practical and vocational skills are low in the hierarchy. It is here between the relationship of the value placed on the hierarchy and importance of educational knowledge that the deeper 'hidden' explanations of the functions of education and the assessment system are found.

Broadfoot (1979) identifies different lines of argument in the analysis of these explanations of the relationships. She contrasts the 'liberal-reformist' ideology based on social liberation and egalitarian ideals against the 'conflict-control' ideology based on repression and social control. However even in the 'liberal-reformist' tradition, the competitive meritocracy results in maintaining the same hierarchy of knowledge and tradition. The 'conflict-control' ideology argues that the system perpetuates existing class and economic relations, and represses and controls through the hierarchy of knowledge in the elite culture. This works in subtle ways so that it is not seen as repression and control. Thus the educational system and assessment reproduces inequalities in society and elitist and middle-class values, and this is obscured through an apparent objectivity in assessment and legitimated through an ideal of merit.

Whatever one believes about these explanations and dominance of the ideologies over the education system, it must be accepted that the traditional assessment system is persistent, and has now been strengthened through the GCSE and the National Curriculum assessments throughout the years of schooling. Even though it appears that the system is becoming in one sense more dysfunctional in relation to selection for employment, that is, with large scale unemployment large numbers of pupils will leave with qualifications but will not be able to get jobs, it is being made more functional in another sense by being emphasized that it is a basic necessary prerequisite to any job and that there is a need for better qualified people in modern society in the types of jobs which are available. It is also strengthened by its use in further and higher education as a selective mechanism for particular courses, and the expansion of this sector.

Departmental and School Assessment Policies

One of the consequences of recent reforms and the emphasis on assessment in the National Curriculum, GCSE and ROA is the need for the development of department and school assessment policies. Perhaps it is not too surprising to read that, a few years ago, in a survey (supported by the NFER) of 112 secondary and middle schools, less than half had a written assessment policy and a third admitted that they had no policy at all and were not developing one at that time, and even fewer (less than one third) had policies at departmental level (Clough, Davis and Sumner, 1984). Moreover only fourteen schools sent in copies of their policy as requested and, in the main, these were fairly basic. By 1991, it seems that developments had been made in the secondary sector but very little progress had been made on this issue in the primary sector, judging by the HM Inspectorate Report (DES, 1991d).

Few primary schools had written specific policies on assessment and recording, although common practices were developing as a result of agreements reached through discussion. Other schools had no stated policy which led to inconsistent practice among teachers. In the secondary sector, policies and practices relating to Records of Achievement were of variable quality and had not been modified to include National Curriculum developments. The purposes of assessment, in particular the value and use of assessment in supporting learning, were not made explicit in over three quarters of assessment, recording and reporting policies. (p. 28)

Of course, the fact that there is no written policy in a school or department does not mean that they are not doing any assessment, or that the assessment practices are poor, or that they are disorganized. They may well be following unwritten policies, and it may be they have just not got round to formalising their everyday practices. Nor does a written policy mean that there is, of necessity, good assessment practice in operation. It is one thing to write a policy and another to effect it in practice. There is no merit in a written policy for its own sake.

Perhaps we should question the need for school and departmental policies first of all. Why have a policy? I think there can be a number of benefits of a good policy which can be supported by research and reports (for example, DES, 1988 and 1991; Clough *et al*, 1984). There are not only the benefits of the policy to consider, but it may be that the process which is gone through to write the policy is just as important as the policy itself. For example, if the policy contains purposes and uses of assessment, as I think a good policy should, then this will involve a departmental discussion on curricular aims, and staff will get a full understanding of what they are doing and what assessment is all about. In a policy assessment is unlikely to be a discrete activity, as it often appears to be at present. This will also mean that teachers will not go in at the 'doing' assessment stage, or even, the later recording assessment stage as they often appear to do at present without a policy. They will not miss the vital, 'knowing what they are doing it for' stage. This way too there should not be as many objections to assessment practices as there are at present. Other main benefits are the co-ordination of assessment across the recent initiatives, National Curriculum, ROA and examinations, continuity in curriculum and recording, and the standardization of practices amongst teachers so that gradings, comments and formats have more meaning to all users, teachers, pupils and parents.

What I am suggesting is that each Head of a PE Department in a secondary school and curriculum leader in the primary, in discussion with colleagues, should draw up an assessment policy as part of their departmental or subject policy. It should, of course, fit in with school policies and LEA guidelines where these exist. It is suggested that a good departmental or subject assessment policy would include statements on the practices and procedures to be followed on many of the issues discussed in this book. These are indicated in table 26. Although this list may seem lengthy, and perhaps daunting to many teachers, it is not designed to make more work for the teachers. It is designed to give more purpose to practice,

Table 26: Elements to be included in a departmental assessment policy

Relation to LEA, and School policy/guidelines.
Relation to curriculum — National Curriculum ES and POS.
Relation to public examinations.
Purposes and uses — Formative and Summative.
What is to be assessed.
Methods of assessment.
Records to be kept.
When assessment and recording is to take place.
The pupils' role in assessment.
The keeping of pupils' work and records.
Grading and marking structures and procedures.
Standardisation procedures.
Reporting to parents.
Equal opportunities — pupils with special needs.
                              gender, ethnic minorities.
Staff induction and training.
Review of policy — how, when.

and to ensure that assessment is more beneficial to both teachers and pupils. As indicated by Clough *et al* (1984), undirected, uncoordinated assessment practices may mean more work, less useful assessment and seem more of a chore than policy-directed practices.

References

ALDERSON, J. (1988) 'Issues and strategies', *National Conference for 'A' Level PE and Sports Studies*, Guildford, AEB.

APU (1983) *Aesthetic Development*, London, APU.

ARMSTRONG, N. (1987) 'A comment on physical fitness testing', *British Journal of Physical Education* (BJPE), 17, 1, p. 34.

ARMSTRONG, N. (1990) 'Childrens' physical activity patterns: The implications for physical education' in ARMSTRONG, N. (Ed) *New Directions in Physical Education Vol 1*, Leeds, Human Kinetics.

ASPIN, D. (1974) 'Sport and the concept of the aesthetic' in WHITING, J. and MASTERSON, D. (Eds) *Readings in the Aesthetics of Sport*, London, Lepus Books.

BALL, S. (1981) *Beechside Comprehensive*, Cambridge, Cambridge University Press.

BALOGH, J. (1982) *Profile Reports for School Leavers*, York, Longman for the Schools Council.

BARNES, D., BRITTEN, J. and ROSEN, H. (1971) *Language, The Learner and The School*, London, Penguin.

BAYLISS, T. (1989) 'PE and racism: Making changes', *Multicultural Teaching*, 7, 2, pp. 19–22.

BBC1 (1987) *Panorama*, TV programme, March.

BCPE (1989) *Physical Education for Ages 5–16: A Framework for Discussion*, London, BCPE.

BEASHELL, P. and TAYLOR, J. (1986) *Sport Examined*, London, MacMillan.

BEASHELL, P. and TAYLOR, J. (1988) *Sport Assignments*, London, MacMillan.

BERNSTEIN, B. (1972) 'On the classification and framing of educational knowledge', in YOUNG, M.F.D. (Ed) *Knowledge and Control*, London, Collier-MacMillan.

BEST, D. (1974) 'The aesthetic in sport', *British Journal of Aesthetics*, 15, 3.

BIRD, C. (1980) 'Deviant labelling in schools: The pupils' perspective', in WOODS, P. (Ed) *Pupil Strategies*, London, Croom Helm.

BJPE (1989) Number of articles, *BJPE*, 20, 1.

BLOOM, B.S. (1956) *Taxonomy of Educational Objectives: The Cognitive Dimension* New York, McKay.

BLUMER, H. (1971) 'Sociological implications of the thought of George Herbert Mead', in COSIN, E.R. *et al* (Eds) *School and Society*, London, RKP.

BOARD OF EDUCATION (1943) *Curriculum and Examinations in Secondary Schools* (The Norwood Report), London, HMSO.

BOOTON, P. (1986) 'One form of assessment', *Bulletin of Physical Education*, 22, pp. 32–42.

BOSCO, J.S. and GUSTAFSON, W.R. (1983) *Measurement and Evaluation in Physical Education, Fitness and Sports*, Englewood-Cliffs, NJ, Prentice Hall.

BROADFOOT, P. (1979) *Assessment, Schools and Society*, London, Methuen.

BROWN, B. (1990) 'The administration of GCSE: An outline', in RIDING, R. and BUTTERFIELD, S. (Eds) *Assessment and Examinations in the Secondary Schools*, London, Routledge.

BULLETIN OF PE (1986) Number of articles, *Bulletin of PE*, 22.

CAMERON, R. (1991) 'Curriculum related assessment: The importance of educationally relevant data', in HARDING, L. and BEECH, J.R. (Eds) *Educational Assessment of the Primary School Child*, Windsor, NFER-Nelson.

CARRINGTON, B. and WILLIAMS, T. (1988) 'Patriarchy and ethnicity: The link between school physical education and community leisure activities' in EVANS, J. (Ed) *Teachers, Teaching and Control in Physical Education*, Lewes, Falmer Press.

CARRINGTON, B. and WOOD, R. (1983) 'Body-talk: Images of sport in a multiracial school', *Multi Racial Education*, 11, 2, pp. 29–38.

CARROLL, B. (1976a) 'Physical education teachers evaluations of their own lessons', *Journal of Psycho-Social Aspects of Human Movement*, 2, pp. 30–9.

CARROLL, B. (1976b) 'PE teachers' assessment of pupils', paper at *Sociology of PE Workshop*, University of Manchester.

CARROLL, B. (1980) 'Objectives and evaluation in physical education', *Scottish Journal of PE*, 8, 1, pp. 16–21.

CARROLL, B. (1982) 'Examinations and curriculum change in physical education', *Physical Education Review*, 5, 1, pp. 26–36.

CARROLL, B. (1986a) 'Examinations in physical education: An analysis of trends and developments', in *Trends and Developments in Physical Education*. Conference papers of the V111 Commonwealth and International Conference on Sport, PE, Dance, Recreation and Health, London, E and F.N. Spon.

CARROLL, B. (1986b) 'Troublemakers: Making a name in physical education: A study of a label' in EVANS, J. (Ed) *Physical Education, Sport and Schooling*, Lewes, Falmer, Press.

CARROLL, B. (1986c) 'What's in a name? Pupils' identity in physical education', *PE Review*, 9, 1, pp. 19–27.

CARROLL, B. (1990a) 'Examinations and assessment in physical education', in ARMSTRONG, N. (Ed) *New Directions in Physical Education. Vol 1*, Leeds. Human Kinetics.

CARROLL, B. (1990b) 'The twain shall meet: GCSE and the National Curriculum', *BJPE*, 21, 3, pp. 29–32.

CARROLL, B. (1991) 'The National Curriculum and GCSE: Relationship and issues', *PEA Conference on Examinations and the National Curriculum*, Sheffield.

CARROLL, B. (1993) 'Physical education: Challenges and responses to cultural diversity', in PUMFREY, P.D. and VERMA, G.K. (Eds) *Cultural Diversity and the Curriculum, Vol. 1. The Foundation Subjects and Religious Education in Secondary Schools*, London, Falmer Press.

CARROLL, B. and HOLLINSHEAD, G. (1993a) 'Equal opportunities: Race and gender in physical education', in EVANS, J. (Ed) *Equality, Education and Physical Education*. London, Falmer Press.

CARROLL, B. and HOLLINSHEAD, G. (1993b) 'Ethnicity and conflict in physical education', *British Educational Research Journal*, 19, 1, pp. 59–76.

CCPR (1992) *Physical Education in Primary Schools — A sporting chance?* London, CCPR.

CLOUGH, E., DAVIS, P. and SUMNER, R. (1984) *Assessing Pupils: A Study of Policy on Practice*, Windsor, NFER-Nelson.

COHEN, S. (1972) *Folk Devils and Moral Panics*, London, MacGibbon and Kee.

DEPARTMENT OF EDUCATION FOR NORTHERN IRELAND (1991) *Physical Education: Programmes of Study and Attainment Targets*, Belfast. HMSO.

DES (1984) *Records of Achievement: A Statement of Policy*, London, HMSO.

DES (1985) *Education For All.* (The Swann Report) London, HMSO.

DES (1988) *Records of Achievement. Report of the National Evaluation Pilot Schemes (PRAISE)*, London, HMSO.

DES (1989a) *Records of Achievement. Report of the ROA National Steering Committee (RANSC)*, London, HMSO.

DES (1989b) *National Curriculum. From Policy to Practice*, London, DES.

DES (1991a) *National Curriculum Physical Education, Working Group: Interim Report*, London, DES.

DES (1991b) *Physical Education for ages 5 to 16.* (Final report of the working group) Proposals of the Secretary of State for Education and Science and Secretary of State for Wales, London, DES.

DES (1991c) *The Teaching and Learning of Physical Education: HM Inspection Review: Aspects of Primary Education*, London, HMSO.

DES (1991d) *Assessment, Recording, Reporting: A Report by HM. Inspectorate for the first year 1989–90*, London, DES.

DES (1992) *Physical Education in the National Curriculum.* (Statutory Orders). London, HMSO.

DOUGLAS, J.W.B. (1964) *The Home and the School*, London, MacGibbon and Kee.

EMPLOYMENT DEPT. (1991) *Recording Achievement and Planning Individual Development: Guidance on Summarising the Record and Completing the National Record of Achievement*, London, Employment Dept.

EOC (1988) 'National testing and equal opportunities', in TGAT Report. (appendix F) *National Curriculum: A Report from Task Group on Assessment and Testing*, London, DES.

EVANS, J. (1976) 'An argument against examinations', *BJPE*, 7, 1, p. 110.

EVANS, J. (1984) 'Muscle, sweat and showers: Girls conceptions of physical education and sport: A challenge for research and curriculum reform', *PE Review*, 7, 1, pp. 12–18.

EVANS, J. (1989) 'Swinging from the crossbar: Equality and opportunity in the physical education curriculum', *BJPE*, 20, 2, pp. 86–7.

EVANS, W. and BROLL, B. (1992) 'A new approach to schemes of work for physical education', *BJPE*, 23, 1, pp. 33–5.

FAIRBAIRN, D.J. (1988) 'Pupil profiling: New approaches to recording and reporting achievement', in MURPHY, R. and TORRANCE, H. (Eds) *The Changing Face of Educational Assessment*, Milton Keynes, Open University Press.

FENTEM, P.H., BASSEY, E.J. and TURNBULL, N.B. (1988) *The New Case for Exercise*, London, Sports Council and Health Education Authority.

FLEMING, S. (1991) 'Sport, schooling and Asian male youth culture', in JARVIE, G. (Ed) *Sport, Racism and Ethnicity*, Lewes, Falmer Press.

FLINTOFF, A. (1990) 'Physical education, equal opportunities and the National Curriculum: Crisis or challenge', *PE Review*, 13, 2, pp. 85–100.

FLINTOFF, A. (1991) 'Dance, masculinity and teacher education', *BJPE*, 22, 4, pp. 31–5.

FOX, K. (1992) 'Education for exercise and the National Curriculum proposals: A step forwards or backwards?', *BJPE*, 23, 1, pp. 8–11.

FOX, K. and BIDDLE, S. (1986) 'Health related fitness testing in schools', *Bulletin of PE*, 22, 3, pp. 54–64.

FOX, K. and BIDDLE, S. (1987) 'Health related fitness testing in schools', *Bulletin of PE,* 23, 1, pp. 28–39.

FOX, K. and BIDDLE, S. (1988) 'The child's perspective in PE — Childrens' participation motives', *BJPE*, 19, 2, pp. 79–82.

FRANCIS, J. (1988) 'Examinations at 'A' level GCE in PE and Sport Studies: The current situation', *BJPE*, 19, 6, pp. 212–3.

FRANCIS, J. (1990) ' "A" level examinations in PE and Sports Studies — Open to all', *BJPE*, 21, 3, pp. 338–40.

References

FRANCIS, J. (1992) 'The growth, development and future of PE and Sports Studies at advanced level GCE', *BJPE*, 23, 1, pp. 35–7.

GCSE (1986–92) Syllabuses, Reports LEAG, MEG, SEG, NEA, WJEC, NISEAC.

GIPPS, C. (1990) *Assessment: A Teacher's Guide to the Issues*, London, Hodder and Stoughton.

GLEW, P. (1983) 'Are your fixtures really necessary?', *BJPE*, 14, 4, pp. 100–1.

HAMMERSLEY, M. (1974) 'The organisation of pupil participation', *Sociological Review*, 22, pp. 355–68.

HARGREAVES, A. (1989) *Curriculum and Assessment Reform*, Milton Keynes, Open University Press.

HARGREAVES, D.H. (1967) *Social Relations in a Secondary School*, London, RKP.

HARGREAVES, D.H. (1982) 'Ten proposals for the future of PE', *The Bulletin of PE*, 13, pp. 5–10.

HARGREAVES, D.H., HESTER, S.K. and MELLOR, F.J. (1975) *Deviance in Classrooms*, London, RKP.

HARRIS, J. (1988) 'A health focus in PE' in ALMOND, L. (Ed) *The Place of Physical Education in Schools*, London, Kogan Page.

HARRIS, J. and ELBOURN, J. (1992) 'Highlighting health related exercise within the National Curriculum', *BJPE*, 23, 1, pp. 18–22.

HARROW, A.J. (1972) *A Taxonomy of the Psychomotor Domain*, New York, Longman.

HATFIELD, S.C. and PHILLIPS, R. (1989) *Records of Achievement in Physical Education*, *Topic No. 3*, NWCPEA.

HENDRY, L.B. (1975) 'Survival in a marginal role: The professional identity of the PE teacher', *British Journal of Sociology*, XXVI, 4, 11, pp. 465–76.

HENDRY, L.B. (1978) *School, Sport and Leisure*, London, Lepus Books.

HOWARD, K. and LAWS, C. (1989) 'Where is aesthetic education in physical education', *BJPE*, 20, 3, pp. 126–8.

HUDSON, L. (1966) *Contrary Imaginations*, London, Penguin.

HUMBERSTONE, B. (1990) 'The National Curriculum and outdoor education: Implications and dilemmas', *BJPE*, 21, 1, pp. 244–6.

ITV CHANNEL 4 (1992) *Dispatches*, TV Programme, 5 February.

JACKSON, B. and MARSDEN, D. (1962) *Education and the Working Class*, London, Routledge and Kegan Paul.

JACKSON, P.W. (1968) *Life in Classrooms*, New York, Holt, Rinehart and Winston.

JEPSON, J. and CARROLL, B. (1991) 'RDA v reports: What the pupils say', *BJPE*, 22, 2, pp. 19–22.

JONES, B.A. (1990) 'Assessing the effects of a course in health related fitness in changing the attitudes of pupils towards curriculum physical education', *BJPE, Research Supplement*, 8, pp. 24–7.

KANE, J.E. (1974) *Physical Education in Secondary Schools*, London, MacMillan.

KEDDIE, N. (1971) 'Classroom knowledge', in YOUNG, M.F.D. (Ed) *Knowledge and Control*, London, Collier MacMillan.

KELLY, G.A. (1955) *The Psychology of Personal Constructs*, New York, Norton.

KELLY, M. (1986) 'The use of skills and sports awards in physical education in the 8–14 age group, M.Ed dissertation, University of Manchester.

KINGDON, M. and STOBART, G. (1987) *GCE Examined*, Lewes, Falmer Press.

KIRK, D. (1984) 'Physical education, aesthetics and education', *PE Review*, 7, 1, pp. 65–72.

LACEY, C. (1970) *Hightown Grammar*, Manchester, Manchester University Press.

LAVENTURE, B. (1992) 'School to community — Progress and partnership' in ARMSTRONG, N. (Ed) *New Directions in Physical Education, Vol 2*, Leeds, Human Kinetics.

LEAMAN, O. (1984) *Sit on the Sidelines and Watch the Boys Play: Sex Differentiation in Physical Education*, London, Longman.

MacConachie-Smith, J. (1991) 'Assessment of progression in National Curriculum physical education', *BJPE*, 22, 2, pp. 11–15.

MacIntosh, H.G. (1974) *Techniques and Problems of Assessment*, London, Edward Arnold.

Mackrell, G.I. (1987) 'Records of Achievement — An Employer's Viewpoint,' *In Profile*, 1, 6, p. 1, Tunbridge Wells, SERA.

McNamee, M. (1990) 'Assessment and attainment: Physical education and the National Curriculum', *BJPE*, 21, 1, pp. 233–5.

Mangan, J.A. (1973) 'Some sociological concomitants of secondary school physical education: Exploratory suggestions', in Mangan, J.A. (Ed) *Physical Education and Sport: Sociological and Cultural Perspectives*, Oxford, Basil Blackwell.

Marsden, R.J. (1990) 'Meeting the challenge of 'A' level Sport Studies', *BJPE*, 21, 3, pp. 35–6.

Meakin, D.C. (1980) 'Aesthetic appraisal and human movement', *PE Review*, 3, 1, pp. 41–9.

Meek, G. (1991) 'Mainstreaming physical education' in Armstrong, N. and Sparkes, A. (Eds) *Issues in Physical Education*, London, Cassell.

Mosston, M. (1986) *Teaching Physical Education*, Toronto, Merill.

Munby, S. (1989) *Assessing and Recording Achievement*, Oxford, Blackwell.

Murdoch, E. (1990) 'Physical education and sport: The interface' in Armstrong, N. (Ed) *New Directions in Physical Education Vol 1*, Leeds, Human Kinetics.

Murphy, C. (1990) 'Who'd tackle GCSE PE?', *BJPE*, 21, 3, pp. 341–3.

Murphy, P. (1989) 'Assessment and gender', *NUT Review*, 3, 2.

Musgrove, F. and Taylor, P.H. (1969) *Society and the Teacher's Role*, London, Routledge and Kegan Paul.

Nash, R. (1973) *Classroom Observed*, London, RKP.

NCC (1991) *Consultation Report. Physical Education*, York, NCC.

NCC (1992) *Physical Education. Non-Statutory Guidance*, York, NCC.

Newsom Report (1963) *Half Our Future*, London, HMSO.

Nicholas, S. (1990) 'Starting "A" level PE', *BJPE*, 21, 3, p. 344.

Papaioannou, A. (1992) 'Students' motivation in physical education classes, perceived to have different goal perspectives', Phd thesis, University of Manchester.

Peel, E.A. (1971) *The Nature of Adolescent Judgement*, London, Staples Press.

Phillips, P. (1989) 'The students' perspective — some warnings and concerns', in Munby, S. (Ed) *Assessing and Recording Achievement*, Oxford, Blackwell.

Pollard, A. (1988) 'Physical education, competition and control in primary education', in Evans, J. (Ed) *Teachers, Teaching and Control in Physical Education*, Lewes, Falmer Press.

Pollitt, A., Entwistle, N., Hutchinson, C. and De Leica, C. (1985) *What Makes Exam Questions Difficult?*, Edinburgh, Scottish Academic Press.

Rosenthal, R. and Jacobson, L. (1968) *Pygmalion in the Classroom*, New York, Holt, Rinehart & Winston.

Rowntree, D. (1977) *Assessing Students. How Shall We Know Them?*, London, Harper and Row.

Roy, W. (1986) *The New Examination System*, London, Croom Helm.

Satterly, D. (1989) *Assessment in Schools*, (2nd edn), Oxford, Basil Blackwell.

School Sport Forum (1988) *Sport and Young People: Partnership in Action*, London, Sports Council.

Schools Council (1977) *Examinations in Physical Education: A Report of the Working Party of the Schools Council PE Committee*, London, Schools Council.

Schools Council (1981) *Examinations in Physical Education and Related Areas*, London, Schools Council.

Scraton, S.J. (1986) 'Images of feminity in the teaching of girls' physical education', in Evans, J. (Ed) *Physical Education, Sport and Schooling*, Lewes, Falmer Press.

References

SCRE (1977) *Pupils in Profile*, Edinburgh, SCRE.

SELKIRK, K. (1988) *Assessment at 16*, London, Routledge.

SERA (1987) *In Profile*, 1, 6, SERA.

SHA (1990) *Enquiry into Provision of Physical Education in Secondary Schools*, London, SHA.

SHERIDAN, W. (1974) 'Open-ended questions', in MACINTOSH, H.G. (Ed) *Techniques and Problems of Assessment*, London, Edward Arnold.

SKELTHORNE, A. (1986) 'The development of a profiling system', *Bulletin of PE*, 22, pp. 43–7.

SKINSLEY, M. (1986) 'Profiling using the computer', *Bulletin of PE*, 22, pp. 48–51.

SKINSLEY, M. (1987) 'Computer assisted fitness testing', *BJPE*, 18, 6, pp. 276–7.

SLEAP, M. (1990) 'Promoting health in primary schools physical education' in ARMSTRONG, N. (Ed) *New Directions in Physical Education*, Leeds, Human Kinetics.

SMITH, B. (1989) 'Curriculum developments in gymnastics' in ALMOND, L. (Ed) *The Place of Physical Education in Schools*, London, Kogan Page.

SNAILHAM, G.J. (1990) 'A survey of fitness testing in secondary schools in a selected area of Lancashire', unpublished MEd project, Manchester University.

SPARKES, A. (1991a) 'Curriculum change: On gaining a sense of perspective', in ARMSTRONG, N. and SPARKES, A. (Eds) *Issues in Physical Education*, London, Cassell.

SPARKES, A. (1991b) 'Alternative visions of health related fitness: An exploration of problem setting and its consequences', in ARMSTRONG, N. and SPARKES, A. (Eds) *Issues in Physical Education*, London, Cassell.

SPORTS COUNCIL (1991) *Provision for Swimming*, London, Sports Council.

SSEC (1963) *The Certificate of Secondary Education: Some Suggestions for Teachers and Examiners*. SSEC Bulletin No. 1, London, HMSO.

SUGDEN, D. (1991) 'Assessment of children with movement skill difficulties', *BJPE*, 22, 2, pp. 16–18.

SWALES, T. (1979) *Record of Personal Achievement : An Independent Evaluation of the Swindon RPA Scheme*, (Pamphlet 16), London, Schools Council.

TALBOT, M. (1990) 'Equal opportunities and physical education', in ARMSTRONG, N. (Ed) *New Directions in Physical Education Vol 1*, Leeds, Human Kinetics.

THOMAS, W.I. (1928) *The Child in America*, New York, Knopf.

THORPE, R. and BUNKER, D. (1989) 'A changing focus in games teaching', in ALMOND, L. (Ed) *The Place of Physical Education in Schools*, London, Kogan Page.

UNDERWOOD, G.L. (1983) *The Physical Education Curriculum: Planning and Implementation*, Lewes, Falmer Press.

VEAL, M.L. (1988) 'Pupil assessment perceptions and practices of secondary teachers', *Journal of Teaching in Physical Education*, 7, pp. 327–42.

WALTERS, D. (1991) 'A theoretical analysis of GCSE physical education practical assessment criteria', *BJPE*, 22, 2, pp. 23–6.

WARD, E. and HARDMAN, K. (1978) 'The influence of values on the role perception of men physical education teachers', *PE Review*, 1, 1, pp. 59–65.

WHITE, D.R. and HARVEY, N.G. (1980) *Exceptional Teaching*, Columbus, OH, Merrill.

WILLIAMS, J.L. (1986) 'Public examinations in dance', in *The Study of Dance and the Place of Dance in Society*. Conference papers of the VIII Commonwealth and International Conference on Sport, PE, Dance, Recreation and Health, London, E. and F.N. Span.

WILMUT, J. (1988) 'An evaluation of the 2nd year of the course in Sports Studies at advanced level', *AEB Conference*, Guildford, AEB.

WILSON, J. (1986) 'Assessing aesthetic appreciation: A review', in ROSS, M. (Ed) *Assessment in Arts Education*, Oxford, Pergamon Press.

WOLFENDEN COMMITTEE ON SPORT (1960) *Sport in the Community*, London, CCPR.

WOOD, J.S. (1981) 'Physical education teachers' labelling from the pupils' perspective', M. Ed, dissertation, University of Manchester.

WOOLLAM, S. (1978) 'The case against examinations', in BCPE Report of Conference on *Assessment of Physical Education in Schools and Colleges. BCPE.*

Appendix: Useful Addresses

Examining Groups

London and East Anglian Examining Group (LEAG)
now called University of London Examinations and Assessment Council (ULEAC)

The Lindens,
139 Lexden Road,
Colchester, CO3 3RL.
Tel. 0206 549595

Midland Examining Group (MEG)

West Midlands Examinations Board,
Mill Wharf,
Mill Street,
Birmingham, B6 4BU.
Tel. 021 628 2000

Northern Examining Association (NEA)
now called Northern Examinations and Assessment Board (NEAB)

31–33 Springfield Avenue
Harrogate
Yorkshire, HG1 2HW

Southern Examining Group (SEG)

Guildford Office,
Stag Hill House,
Guildford, GU2 5XJ.
Tel. 0483 506506

Welsh Joint Examination Committee (WJEC)

245 Western Avenue,
Cardiff, CF5 2YX.
Tel. 0222 561231

Northern Ireland Schools Examinations and Assessment Council (NISEAC)

Beechill House,
42 Beechill Road,
Belfast, BT8 4RS.
Tel. 0232 704666

Associated Examining Board (AEB)

Stag Hill House,
Guildford, GU2 5XJ
Tel. 0483 506506

Scottish Examination Board

Ironmills Road,
Dalkeith,
Midlothian, EH22 1LE.
Tel. 031 663 6601

Vocational Qualifications

City and Guilds of London Institute (CLGI, C&G)

46 Britannia Street,
London, WC1X 9RG.
Tel. 071 278 2468

Business and Technology Education Council (BTEC)

Central House
Upper Woburn Place
London, WC1H 0HH
Tel. 071 413 8400

National Council for Vocational Qualifications (NCVQ)

222 Euston Road
London, NW1 2BZ
Tel. 071 387 9898

Other Addresses

Schools Examinations and Assessment Council (SEAC)

Newcombe House,
45 Notting Hill Gate,
London, W11 3JB.
Tel. 081 229 1234

Appendix: Useful Addresses

National Curriculum Council (NCC)

Albion Wharf,
25 Skeldergate,
York, YO1 2XL.
Tel. 0904 622533

Index